WILLIAM CONGREVE

The Way of the World

Edited by

KATHLEEN M. LYNCH

EDWARD ARNOLD

Regents Restoration Drama Series

The Regents Restoration Drama Series, similar in objectives and format to the Regents Renaissance Drama Series, will provide soundly edited texts, in modern spelling, of the more significant English plays of the late seventeenth and early eighteenth centuries. The word "Restoration" is here used ambiguously and must be explained. If to the historian it refers to the period between 1660 and 1685 (or 1688), it has long been used by the student of drama in default of a more precise word to refer to plays belonging to the dramatic tradition established in the 1660's, weakening after 1700, and displaced in the 1730's. It is in this extended sense—imprecise though justified by academic custom—that the word is used in this series, which will include plays first produced between 1660 and 1737. Although these limiting dates are determined by political events, the return of Charles II (and the removal of prohibitions against the operation of theaters) and the passage of Walpole's Stage Licensing Act, they enclose a period of dramatic history having a coherence of its own in the establishment, development, and disintegration of a tradition.

Each text in the series is based on a fresh collation of the seventeenth- and eighteenth-century editions that might be presumed to have authority. The textual notes, which appear above the rule at the bottom of each page, record all substantive departures from the edition used as the copy-text. Variant substantive readings among contemporary editions are listed there as well. Editions later than the eighteenth century are referred to in the textual notes only when an emendation originating in some one of them is received into the text. Variants of accidentals (spelling, punctuation, capitalization) are not recorded in the notes. Contracted forms of characters' names are silently expanded in speech prefixes and stage directions, and, in the case of speech prefixes, are regularized. Additions to the stage directions of the copy-text are enclosed in brackets. Stage directions such as "within" or "aside" are enclosed in parentheses when they occur in the copy-text.

Spelling has been modernized along consciously conservative lines, but within the limits of a modernized text the linguistic quality of the original has been carefully preserved. Punctuation has been brought into accord with modern practices. The objective has been to achieve a balance between the generally light pointing of the old editions, and a system of punctuation which, without overloading the text with exclamation marks, semicolons, and dashes, will make the often loosely flowing verse and prose of the original syntactically intelligible to the modern reader. Dashes are regularly used only to indicate interrupted speeches, or shifts of address within a single speech.

Explanatory notes, chiefly concerned with glossing obsolete words and phrases, are printed below the textual notes at the bottom of each page. References to stage directions in the notes follow the admirable system of the Revels editions, whereby stage directions are keyed, decimally, to the line of the text before or after which they occur. Thus, a note on 0.2 has reference to the second line of the stage direction at the beginning of the scene in question. A note on 115.1 has reference to the first line of the stage direction following line 115 of the text of the relevant scene. Speech prefixes, and any stage directions attached to them, are keyed to the first line of accompanying dialogue.

JOHN LOFTIS

Stanford University

Contents

Introduction

The present edition of *The Way of the World* is based on the first
quarto (Q1), published in 1700. The second quarto (Q2), published
in 1706, was set from the first quarto and does not substantially differ
from it. There are some minor improvements, as well as minor errors,
in spelling and punctuation in Q2; but in Q2 the regularizing of
Mincing's illiterate language must be deplored, and phrases which are
by no means redundant are carelessly omitted. In the 1710 edition of
Congreve's collected works (W1) the text of *The Way of the World*
was set from Q2, repeats its omissions and some of its unjustified
changes, and corrects certain errors. In W1 new scenes are indicated
within the acts for the first time, following the French convention, at
the entrance or exit of characters. The textual notes of the present
edition give variants from Q1 which appear in Q2 and in W1.

The Way of the World was somewhat coolly received when it was
first acted at Lincoln's Inn Fields Theatre, probably in the first
week of March, 1700. Dryden wrote to Mrs. Steward on March 12:
"Congreve's new play has had but moderate success, though it
deserves much better."[1] On the same day Lady Marow wrote to an
acquaintance in the country that "Congreve's new play doth not
answer expectation, there being no plot in it but many witty things to
ridicule the Chocolate House, and the fantastical part of the world."[2]
Downes attributed the fact that the play "had not the success the
company expected" to the fact that it was "too keen a satire."[3]
Congreve himself acknowledged in his *Dedication* that he had scarcely
expected the play to succeed, "for but little of it was prepared for
that general taste which seems now to be predominant in the palates
of an audience." He resolved to "commit his quiet and his fame

---

[1] John Dryden, *Letters*, ed. Charles E. Ward (Durham, North Carolina,
1942), p. 134.

[2] Historical MSS. Commission, *Dartmouth*, III, 145.

[3] John Downes, *Roscius Anglicanus*, ed. Montague Summers (London,
n.d.), p. 45.

no more to the caprices of an audience"[4] and retired from the stage at the early age of thirty. Had Dryden not died in May of that year, it is possible that, as Congreve's "true lover," he might have dissuaded his brilliant disciple from so drastic a decision.

For its première *The Way of the World* had an excellent cast. Anne Bracegirdle, for whom, as for his other heroines, Congreve had created the role of leading lady, "performing her part so exactly and just, gained the applause of court and city."[5] She presumably again played Millamant (although the cast is not known) in the 1705 revival of the play. Cibber recorded that when she acted Millamant "all the faults, follies, and affectations of that agreeable tyrant were venially melted down into so many charms and attractions of a conscious beauty."[6] Mrs. Bracegirdle was well matched with John Verbruggen as Mirabell. When the pair acted in Aphra Behn's *The Rover*, audiences were enchanted by his "untaught airs" and her "smiling repartees" and "were afraid they were going off the stage every moment."[7] Thomas Betterton, nearing retirement, must have played Fainall with the flamboyant vigor which always distinguished his acting. The original cast included Elizabeth Barry as Marwood, effectively drawling out her words, William Bowen, "an actor of spirit," as Witwoud, and Cave Underhill, who had been D'Avenant's best comedian, as corpulent and awkward Sir Wilfull.

The Way of the World was only sporadically revived for some years and continued to be surpassed in popularity by two of Congreve's other plays, *The Old Bachelor* and *Love for Love*. Slowly, however, "the most intellectually accomplished of English comedies" gained an honorable place in the repertories of the London theaters. Such able actresses as Anne Oldfield, Christiana Horton, Hannah Pritchard, Peg Woffington, and Frances Abington graced the role of Millamant and often chose *The Way of the World* for their benefit performances. Robert Wilks, debonair and genteel, excelled as Mirabell, Colley Cibber as Witwoud, Richard Yates as Sir Wilfull. After 1777 none of Congreve's plays held the stage with success, and

[4] Samuel Johnson, *Lives of the English Poets*, ed. George Birkbeck Hill (Oxford, 1905), II, 224.

[5] Downes, p. 45.

[6] Colley Cibber, *An Apology for the Life of Mr. Colley Cibber*, ed. Robert W. Lowe (London, 1889), I, 173.

[7] [John Genest], *Some Account of the English Stage* (Bath, 1833), II, 380–381.

their performance became infrequent.[8] Two of the plays, *Love for Love* and *The Way of the World*, have fared better in the twentieth century than for many years previously, with notable revivals in both England and America. In the late autumn of 1924 *The Way of the World* had its longest run—one hundred and twenty performances— at the Cherry Lane Theater in New York.

In varying aspects Congreve's drama is always richly reminiscent of earlier drama. In *The Way of the World* the influence of Elizabethan tradition is considerably more diluted than in *Love for Love*, and the influence of Molière is less marked than in *The Double Dealer*. Although certain specific borrowings are made from both sources, *The Way of the World* remains essentially the superlative expression of the courtly mode initiated in pre-Restoration court drama and sustained and enhanced by Congreve's precursors in Restoration comedy.

In a subplot which has important bearings on the main action, *The Way of the World* revives a phase of the intrigue in Ben Jonson's *The Devil is an Ass* (1616). Fitzdottrel and Fainall both treat their wives unfairly and are disposed to desert them for other women. Both wives have lovers who champion their interests and who reduce the husbands to a state of financial dependence on these abused mates. In Jonson's comedy Wittipol secures Fitzdottrel's estate for Frances by causing the unsuspecting Fitzdottrel to convey it in trust to Manly, Wittipol's good friend. In *The Way of the World* Mrs. Fainall had the foresight to give her estate in trust to Mirabell before her marriage with Fainall. Toward the close of each play the husband is suddenly informed of the financial authority with which the signing of the deed has invested his wife, and the wife's security in this matter brings about the husband's surrender and effects a *modus vivendi* for all parties. The Elizabethan influence is also conspicuous in the portrait of Sir Wilfull Witwoud, the boorish country rustic, representing a type that throughout the Restoration period continued to offset the elegance of the city gallant.

In a general way certain characters and certain scenes in *The Way of the World* owe a debt to Molière. The role of Waitwell resembles

---

[8] For an illuminating account of the stage history thus briefly outlined see Emmett L. Avery, *Congreve's Plays on the Eighteenth-Century Stage* (New York, 1951).

that of Mascarille in *Les Précieuses Ridicules*, although Waitwell's courtship of Lady Wishfort is much more condensed than Mascarille's similar exploit. Lady Wishfort's pert maid Foible is in the tradition of Molière's saucy soubrettes, and there is a parallel between the relations of lumpish Peg and her mistress and those of Andrée and the Countess in *La Comtesse d'Escarbagnas*.

Comparisons are often made between *The Way of the World* and *Le Misanthrope*, in which masterpiece Molière is more preoccupied than elsewhere with the tyranny of fashionable society and offers no remedy for its encroachments. Célimène and Millamant have no equals in all the arts of coquetry. In the quarrels of Millamant and Marwood and Célimène and Arsinoé the two younger women deprecate with similar irony their unassailable advantages of youthful charm. It is true that in *Le Misanthrope* Molière permits "the way of the world" to pose a more serious threat to sensible living than in any of his other plays. Yet Célimène, heartless at twenty, seems likely to remain so; Alceste's indignant strictures against the beau monde cannot be laughed away; and the compliant and urbane Philinte cuts a rather sorry figure.

Common sense, so violated in *Le Misanthrope*, remains Molière's comic standard of judgment. By its terms he defines folly and gives wisdom its due. He exposes folly and wishes, whenever possible, to cure it; whereas Congreve, also exposing folly, has not the slightest corrective intention. Congreve's laughter at fools is good-natured; he enjoys them. They are ridiculous because they play the social game unintelligently or extravagantly. They mean well and are usually harmless people in a world where good taste, rather than good sense, is the mark of a disciplined life. With Molière all affectation is folly. Congreve reserves a milder laughter for the intelligent, sensitive, but still affected gentlemen and ladies who constitute his ideal of social excellence, who play the social game with perfect dexterity, with complete grace, but at the expense of their humanity. For the art of being civilized is, after all, a delicious fiction, an amazing make-believe, denying those normal human emotions which sooner or later must intrude and must be reckoned with. Like the Restoration dramatists who preceded him and unlike Molière, Congreve limited his world to an artificial society, the vagaries of which he pretty thoroughly explored.

Declining to adapt himself to the sentimental vogue in comedy which Colley Cibber was popularizing, Congreve chose to follow the literary conventions which had been initiated at the court of Charles I and which, in brighter patterns, had delighted the court of Charles II. The *précieuse* code of etiquette, introduced from France to please the French tastes of Queen Henrietta Maria, had for many years determined the basic requirements of English comedies of manners.[9]

By the rules of that code, briefly stated, a courtship which finally terminates in marriage must be hampered by the hero's lingering relations with other women, which may not be abruptly and rudely broken off. Thus in *The Way of the World* Mirabell must divert Lady Wishfort with the amorous attentions of Sir Rowland, thwart Marwood's jealous scheming, and reconcile the Fainalls before he can win the hand of Millamant. Mirabell's good taste, as he achieves these objectives, is opposed by the extravagant bad taste of Witwoud and Petulant, the rustic gaucherie of Sir Wilfull, and the ill-bred widow-wooing of Waitwell, the servant masquerading as courtier.

Such false wits as Witwoud and Petulant are familiar figures in Restoration comedy. Like Cutter and Worm in Cowley's *The Cutter of Coleman Street* (1661) they are "detracting fops," each disparaging his friend in a burst of confidence to a third party. Cutter privately assures Lucia that Worm is "a good ingenious fellow, that's the truth on't, and a pleasant droll when h'as got a cup o' wine in his pate" but is not to be trusted in serious matters. In a similar confession, Worm explains to Lucia that Cutter is an unreliable fellow, only "he has some wit (to give the devil his due) and that 'tis makes us endure him." In the same spirit, Witwoud confides to Mirabell that Petulant has "a pretty deal of an odd sort of a small wit . . . and if he had but any judgment in the world, he would not be altogether contemptible." And Petulant pays Witwoud back in his own coin by describing him to Mirabell as "soft, you know . . . he's what you call a—what-d'ye-call-'em, a fine gentleman, but he's silly withal." In spite of mutual reservations, Witwoud and Petulant enjoy a congenial camaraderie. They conform to a literary tradition which prescribes their agility in witty raillery.

Mrs. Fainall, loyal to Mirabell, is the least conventional of the "other" women in Mirabell's life. Mrs. Marwood is doomed to failure in her attempts to reclaim a young lover, like Loveit in Etherege's *The Man of Mode* (1676), numerous affected older women

---

9 For a detailed study of the influence of the *précieuse* code see the present editor's *The Social Mode of Restoration Comedy* (New York, 1926).

in the comedies of Thomas Shadwell, and Congreve's own Lady Touchwood in *The Double Dealer*. Lady Wishfort is the old coquette par excellence. Her name and tastes recall Loveit in *The Man of Mode* and Lady Loveyouth in Shadwell's *The Humourists* (1670). Shadwell had created a whole gallery of such portraits. When Lady Wishfort represses her fastidiousness and encourages the grotesque wooing of Sir Rowland, her behavior resembles Beliza's treatment of the vulgar Bernado in Shadwell's *The Amorous Bigot* (1690). Lady Wishfort's pride in the refined education of her daughter, who, however, sadly shames her, parallels Lady Fantast's satisfaction in her ridiculous training of a similar daughter in Shadwell's *Bury Fair* (1689). But Lady Wishfort's characterization is more rounded than that of persons resembling her in earlier comedy. With his usual good humor and perceptiveness, Congreve softens her conventional follies.

In the courtship scenes of *The Way of the World* Congreve followed well-established conventions for railing lovers. Mirabell and Millamant had been presaged by Benedick and Beatrice in Shakespeare's *Much Ado about Nothing* (1599), by Fairfield and Carol in Shirley's *Hyde Park* (1632), and by various lesser lights in Jacobean comedies. Sex duels, often culminating in "proviso" scenes, had long been popular with Restoration dramatists.

The formal proviso scene, in which two lovers frame an argument, item by item, safeguarding with legal precision the freedom of each, had been invented by Honoré D'Urfé in his celebrated codebook of *précieuse* gallantry, *L'Astrée* (1607–1627). D'Urfé's Hylas and Stelle draw up, in the presence of witnesses, a proviso contract insuring their mutual rights of inconstancy. They agree to banish jealousy, respect each other's liberty of speech and action, and abolish in their discourse all terms of endearment. Struck by the comic possibilities of such ostensibly reluctant love-making, Dryden incorporated lively proviso contracts in four of his comedies, *The Wild Gallant* (1663), *Secret Love, or The Maiden Queen* (1667), *Marriage à la Mode* (1672), and *Amphitryon* (1690). Celadon and Florimel in *Secret Love* are so fearful of conjugal boredom that they agree to be married by the "agreeable names" of mistress and gallant, since "the names of husband and wife hold forth nothing, but clashing and cloying, and dullness and faintness in their signification." Proviso scenes took a more farcical turn in James Howard's *All Mistaken, or The Mad Couple* (1667) and Edward Ravenscroft's *The Careless Lovers* (1673) and *The Canterbury Guests* (1694).

In the famous proviso contract of Mirabell and Millamant in the fourth act of *The Way of the World*, Congreve preserved many details of the earlier proviso scenes. Millamant insures her "dear liberty" in carefully detailed provisos. Like Melantha in *Marriage à la Mode* she requests: "Let us never visit together, nor go to a play together." Like Isabelle in *The Wild Gallant*, she describes most of her articles as mere "trifles." She does not, like Florimel, threaten inconstancy, although she insists on the privilege of paying and receiving visits at her pleasure and of writing and receiving letters "without interrogatories or wry faces" on Mirabell's part. Terms of conjugal affection she condemns as emphatically as Celadon and Florimel. She declares that she abhors such names as "wife, spouse, my dear, joy, jewel, love, sweetheart, and the rest of that nauseous cant, in which men and their wives are so fulsomely familiar." Mirabell, like Isabelle's lover, finds her first terms reasonable enough but her later "bill of fare" somewhat alarming.

Mirabell's own provisos, although fairly original, are expressed with all the formality displayed in corresponding scenes in *Secret Love* and in *Amphitryon*. The conventional *imprimis* or *item* introduces each of his articles. In conclusion he concedes: "These provisos admitted, in other things I may prove a tractable and complying husband." With due ceremony he begs leave to kiss Millamant's hand upon the contract. At this moment Mrs. Fainall enters, and Mirabell claims her, as Hillaria in *The Careless Lovers* had claimed her uncle, as a witness to the sealing of the deed. To the end Millamant remains in control of the situation. Quite appropriately she departs from established custom in having her own very characteristic last word:

Well, you ridiculous thing you, I'll have you—I won't be kissed, nor I won't be thanked—here, kiss my hand though.—So, hold your tongue now, and don't say a word.

Congreve had borrowed much, but he improved on what he had borrowed. He achieved the finest of all the proviso scenes in Restoration comedy. The prose of that scene has a poetic luminosity; and the graceful evasiveness of the lovers, sustained with the proper touch of well-bred nonchalance, yields with equal grace to their desired capitulation.

To Jeremy Collier's contemporary invectives against the "immorality and profaneness" of Restoration comedy Congreve somewhat frivolously replied in his *Amendments of Mr. Collier's False and Imperfect Citations* (1698). Collier's attacks seem not to have affected Congreve's literary reputation in that circle of famous men of letters to which he belonged and in which he was highly esteemed. Among his contemporaries perhaps only a few Puritan critics and Congreve himself took exception to Dryden's claim that Heaven had endowed Shakespeare and Congreve equally.[10]

Pope considered Congreve "one of the most valuable men, as well as finest writers of my age and century."[11] Addison ranked "harmonious Congreve"[12] as Dryden's successor. Steele considered that Congreve excelled in "every way of writing."[13] He devoted a whole *Spectator* paper[14] to condemning the corrupt morals of Etherege in *The Man of Mode*, but seems never to have thought of Congreve as belonging to Etherege's school. Dennis, who attacked in venomous fashion most of the men of letters of the day, expressed only unbounded admiration for Congreve. Dennis observed aptly, "most persons" thought, that Congreve "left the stage early, and comedy has quitted it with him."[15]

Nevertheless, the taste of theatergoers had changed, and sophisticated comedy of manners was increasingly subjected to charges of heartlessness and immorality. It is not surprising that Samuel Johnson, the great moral arbiter of his age, felt compelled to decree, as he summed up Congreve's achievement, that "the general tenour and tendency of his plays must always be condemned. It is acknowledged with universal conviction that the perusal of his works will make no man better; and that their ultimate effect is to represent pleasure in alliance with vice, and to relax those obligations by which life ought to be regulated."[16] Yet even Johnson reflected: "Among all the efforts of early genius which literary history records, I doubt whether any one can be produced that more surpasses the common limits of nature than the plays of Congreve."[17] And "one

[10] See Dryden's verses prefixed to *The Double Dealer* (London, 1694).

[11] *The Iliad of Homer Translated by Alexander Pope, Esq.* (London, 1750), Vol. VI, Dedication.

[12] Joseph Addison, *Works* (London, 1721), I, 40.

[13] See Steele's Commendatory Verses "To Mr. Congreve, occasioned by his Comedy called *The Way of the World*."

[14] *The Spectator*, No. 65.

[15] [Giles Jacob], *The Poetical Register* (London, 1719), p. 46.

[16] Johnson, *Lives*, II, 222.

[17] *Ibid.*, p. 219

of the best" of Johnson's "little *Lives*" concludes with the tribute:
"While comedy or while tragedy is regarded Congreve's plays are
likely to be read." [18]

The romantic critics of the nineteenth century took a cautious
delight in Restoration comedy, which they found curiously remote
from the life of their own era. Lamb chose to envisage the world of
Restoration society as released from all laws of time and space, "a
speculative scene of things, which has no reference whatever to the
world that is," a fairy country "beyond the diocese of the strict conscience." [19] Hazlitt was more aware of the historical importance of
dramatists who commemorated "a gala day of wit and pleasure," [20]
among whom he regarded Congreve as by far the wittiest and most
elegant. Leigh Hunt urged that intelligent comprehension of the
manners of an earlier period should stimulate, rather than dismay,
all minds "candidly and healthily trained." [21]

Victorian moral earnestness supplanted this more gracious
approach to Restoration comedy. Macaulay eloquently disparaged
the "exceedingly bad" morality of a beau monde that he found "a
great deal too real" in "everything ridiculous and degrading." [22]
George Meredith, in the very act of assailing the unlovely English
propensity for moralistic judgments, heartily decried the "so-called
comedy of manners" as "comedy of the manners of South-sea islanders
under city veneer; and, as to comic idea, vacuous as the mask without
the face behind it." [23] *The Way of the World*, indeed, Meredith praised
as an exceptional achievement, refusing to recognize that play as a
very perfect example of the mode which he condemned.

In the twentieth century there has been a vigorous revival of
interest in Restoration comedy. Critics have taken a fresh look at
the Restoration tradition, and Congreve has had his rightful share
in that reappraisal. In his admirable and definitive biography,

[18] *Ibid.*, p. 234.

[19] Charles Lamb, *Works*, ed. E. V. Lucas (London, 1903–1905), IV,
142–143.

[20] William Hazlitt, *Works*, ed. A. R. Waller and Arnold Glover (London,
1902–1904), VIII, 70.

[21] *The Dramatic Works of Wycherley, Congreve, Vanbrugh, and Farquhar*, ed.
Leigh Hunt (London and New York, 1866), Preface, p. lxiii.

[22] Thomas Babington Macaulay, *Critical and Historical Essays*, ed. F. C.
Montague (London, 1903), III, 11–12.

[23] George Meredith, *An Essay on Comedy and the Uses of the Comic Spirit*,
ed. Lane Cooper (New York, Chicago, Boston [1918]), p. 83.

William Congreve, the Man (1941), John Hodges demolished Gosse's dull image of Congreve as a man who went through life "as if in felt slippers"[24] and Voltaire's distorted image of Congreve as an elegant trifler. No longer encumbered by moral blinkers, a fair number of modern scholars have dedicated themselves to the rewarding task, initiated by John Palmer, of exploring "a mood of the human spirit which is in every age, though in this particular age it was more conspicuous."[25] Foremost among these scholars has been the humane and gifted English critic Bonamy Dobrée, whose essays on Restoration comedy have been distinguished by a brilliance of style worthy of the subject.

Congreve's plots have been the despair of his admirers, and the plot of *The Way of the World* is no exception. In fact, the ramifications of the intrigues in *The Way of the World* are considerably more difficult to follow than those in *Love for Love* and only a little less confusing than those in *The Double Dealer*. The salient facts of the predicaments that must be resolved in *The Way of the World* are dropped allusively, almost casually, here and there; and when the play is read, a hawk's eye is required to detect them and keep them in order. The close family relationships of the characters and their developing schemes are not easily remembered; and when all threads have been untangled, it appears that nothing is really concluded. It is unlikely that the Fainalls will cease wrangling. Lady Wishfort will continue to hanker for a young lover. Mirabell and Millamant are apprehensive that the constancy for which they long may not be realized.

There is some justice in the complaint that *The Way of the World* is "a series of still-life pictures." Of physical action the play offers only occasional outbursts. Mrs. Marwood turns from Fainall with the threat: "Break my hands, do! I'd leave 'em to get loose." Millamant is on one occasion so "nettled" that she tears her fan. Sir Wilfull, noisily and joyously drunk, shatters throughout a single scene the decorous atmosphere of the drawing room. Lady Wishfort paces the stage in a furious passion and faints with calculated vehemence. But the usual tone of the play is "a harmony of agreeable voices." Despite these handicaps *The Way of the World* acts well.[26] Agreeable voices

---

[24] Edmund Gosse, *Life of William Congreve* (London, 1888), p. 175.

[25] John Palmer, *The Comedy of Manners* (London, 1913), p. 293.

[26] The present editor has had a share in sponsoring three highly successful undergraduate revivals at Mount Holyoke College.

have never been more enchanting, and the gestures that emphasize those flawless cadences make up in precision for what they lack in force.

Toward the end of his life, Congreve remarked that he refrained from "wondering at the world's new wicked ways," and added

> Believe it, men have ever been the same,
> And all the Golden Age is but a dream.[27]

It is ironic that so tolerant an observer of the persistent follies of humanity should have been accused of having created "nothing but a set of heartless fine ladies and gentlemen, coming in and out, saying witty things at each other, and buzzing in some maze of intrigue."[28] Congreve's characters are rounded portraits. The numerous fools have very human qualities, and the thoughtful few have a warmth of feeling which is inconvenient in the beau monde in which they live.

Witwoud and Petulant are eagerly complaisant fops who when united make "one man." Although each delights in using the other as a target for raillery, they "agree in the main, like treble and bass." To "smoke" Sir Wilfull, and especially to "smoke" his boots, gives them a double pleasure because it is a pleasure shared.

Sir Wilfull cannot adorn a London drawing room, but he speaks some homely truths there. In his native Shropshire his hearty manners must have commended him to his friends "round the Wrekin." Baffled by the conventions of polite society, he enjoys, "when a little in disguise," a brief, refreshing respite from its exactions. He is too good-natured to resent Millamant's snubs, offers himself as Mirabell's "fellow traveler," makes a contract with his cousin to help his aunt, and breaks it to make the young lovers happy.

Painted in darker colors, Fainall and Mrs. Marwood are less convincing characters. Mrs. Marwood's bitterness and Fainall's angry resentment seem out of place in an artificial milieu, and the punishment of the two sinners can scarcely be taken seriously. Mrs. Fainall, on the contrary, if only sketched, is one of Congreve's most sympathetic characters. If she had had less stamina, she might have been wrecked by her bad education and hateful marriage; but she

---

[27] *The Mourning Bride, Poems & Miscellanies by William Congreve*, ed. Bonamy Dobrée, World's Classics (Oxford and London [1928]), "Letter, to Viscount Cobham," p. 402.

[28] Leigh Hunt in *The Dramatic Works of Wycherley*, etc., Preface, p. xxx.

remains unembittered, quietly dignified, and a faithful friend to her former lover.

Lady Wishfort is a full-length portrait of the old coquette. We observe her various moods: her spirited encounters with her maids; her indulgence of her nephew; her languishing reception of Sir Rowland; her romantic friendship with Mrs. Marwood; her selfish affection for her daughter; and her plaintive surrender of Mirabell, who "rakes the embers" of a smothered fire in her breast. The contradictions in Lady Wishfort's character are the secret of her extraordinary vitality. Congreve endowed her with a gift of shrewd, cutting irony and a keen sense of humor, which extends to a perception of her own decayed charms, her "arrant ash-color" complexion and her painted face, cracked "like an old peeled wall." "Female frailty!" comments Mrs. Fainall, "we must all come to it, if we live to be old."

Millamant is Congreve's greatest triumph. Her lover, "sententious" Mirabell, is a paler figure than Etherege's Dorimant; but Millamant is the wisest, wittiest, most mature of Restoration coquettes. Other characters in Restoration comedy, even Etherege's Dorimant, have elusive personalities. Although it is apparent that many of these people have warm hearts and generous sympathies, the social mask conceals their best impulses. But through all her subterfuges we know intimately the real Millamant, or at least we boldly fancy so.

Millamant's personality is not exhibited solely through sparkling rejoinders, inspired, from moment to moment, by the wit of her associates. She has a gift for interpreting a situation as a whole and molds her caprices to suit the temper of the occasion. She has an advantage over Mirabell in being able to laugh at his "love-sick face" and mild admonitions, and she gaily exposes the weak spots in his lover's self-conceit. She begs of him in merry concern: "Ha! ha! ha! What would you give that you could help loving me?" And poor Mirabell can only reply: "I would give something that you did not know I could not help it."

Millamant has reflected about marriage. To marry is to relinquish not just one's "dear liberty" but one's separate and individual self. It is to stake all for love—for a love the continuance of which would be a miracle. Where in the circle of her acquaintance has she seen a lasting love? Yet it is in vain that she demurs. Although she maintains her wit and coquetry to the end, her tender, generous, and whole-hearted love for Mirabell is never really obscured in her gay and graceful evasions. She confesses to Mrs. Fainall: "Well, if Mirabell should not make a good husband, I am a lost thing."

Congreve's characters are best revealed in the vivacity of their language. Even the fools contribute to the conquest of dullness. It has been objected that the false wits "are permitted to stumble on too many brilliants." [29] Witwoud's head would be empty if it were not well stocked with similitudes. He is almost breathless in his haste to get them out and is never in better form than when others consent to play the similitude game with him. His flow of similitudes suits his character, as Petulant's snappishness suits his. Lady Wishfort's "boudoir Billingsgate" is a superb invention. Even the servants have their special accents. Foible sweetens impudence with flattery, and Mincing struggles to be genteel.

Millamant's whimsical manner of speech is always unmistakably hers and hers alone. Her very flippancies are charged with meaning. It is plain that her excessive gaiety is forced. She talks very fast and is afraid of pauses, fearful lest the realities of love may somehow rudely intrude upon the pretty decorum of the beau monde. In those inarticulate silences, charged with warmth and color, that check now and again the flashing current of her raillery, Millamant seems wistfully pleading with Mirabell to accept her love without the shame of a confession and to permit her to remain in appearance imperious, brilliant, heartless, the finest of fine ladies.

There has always been unanimity of opinion regarding Congreve's style and particularly regarding its excellence in *The Way of the World*. Hazlitt considered that Congreve attained "the highest model of comic dialogue" and that "there is a peculiar flavour in his very words, which is to be found in hardly any other writer." [30] Dobrée has noted that the melody occasionally heard in *The Double Dealer* and more often in *Love for Love* is pervasive in *The Way of the World*. In Congreve's last comedy a way of life is recorded in matchless prose, with never a false note to mar the interpretation.

KATHLEEN M. LYNCH

Funchal, Madeira

[29] George Henry Nettleton, *English Drama of the Restoration and Eighteenth Century* (New York, 1914), p. 130.
[30] Hazlitt, *Works*, VIII, 71.

Bibliography

Twentieth-Century Studies

AVERY, EMMETT L. *Congreve's Plays on the Eighteenth-Century Stage.* New York, 1951.

DOBRÉE, BONAMY. *Restoration Comedy, 1660–1720.* Oxford, 1924.

FUJIMURA, THOMAS H. *Restoration Comedy of Wit.* Princeton, 1952.

GOSSE, EDMUND. *Life of William Congreve.* London, 1924.

HODGES, JOHN C. *William Congreve, the Man.* New York, 1941.

———, ed. *William Congreve: Letters and Documents.* New York, 1964.

HOLLAND, NORMAN N. *The First Modern Comedies.* Cambridge, Mass., 1959.

KRUTCH, JOSEPH WOOD. *Comedy and Conscience after the Restoration.* New York, 1949.

LOFTIS, JOHN. *Comedy and Society from Congreve to Fielding.* Stanford, 1959.

LYNCH, KATHLEEN M. *The Social Mode of Restoration Comedy.* New York, 1926.

———. *A Congreve Gallery.* Cambridge, Mass., 1951.

MUESCHKE, PAUL and MIRIAM. *A New View of Congreve's Way of the World.* Ann Arbor, Mich., 1958.

NICOLL, ALLARDYCE. *A History of Restoration Drama, 1660–1700.* Fourth edn. Cambridge, 1952.

PALMER, JOHN. *The Comedy of Manners.* London, 1913.

———. *Comedy.* London [1914].

PERRY, HENRY TEN EYCK. *The Comic Spirit in Restoration Drama.* New Haven, 1925.

SMITH, JOHN HARRINGTON. *The Gay Couple in Restoration Comedy.* Cambridge, Mass., 1948.

TAYLOR, D. CRANE. *William Congreve.* London, 1931.

THE WAY OF THE WORLD

COMMENDATORY VERSES

To Mr. Congreve, occasioned by his Comedy called "The Way of the World."

When pleasure's falling to the low delight,
In the vain joys of the uncertain sight;
No sense of wit when rude spectators know,
But in distorted gesture, farce and show;
How could, great author, your aspiring mind   5
Dare to write only to the few refined?
Yet though that nice ambition you pursue,
'Tis not in Congreve's power to please but few.
Implicitly devoted to his fame,
Well-dressed barbarians know his awful name;   10
Though senseless they're of mirth, but when they laugh,
As they feel wine, but when, till drunk, they quaff.
   On you from fate a lavish portion fell
In every way of writing to excel.
Your muse applause to Arabella brings,   15
In notes as sweet as Arabella sings.
Whene'er you draw an undissembled woe,
With sweet distress your rural numbers flow;
Pastora's the complaint of every swain,
Pastora still the echo of the plain!   20
Or if your muse describe, with warming force,
The wounded Frenchman falling from his horse;
And her own William glorious in the strife,
Bestowing on the prostrate foe his life;
You the great act as generously rehearse,   25
And all the English fury's in your verse.
By your selected scenes and handsome choice,
Ennobled Comedy exalts her voice;

0.1 These verses first appeared in W1.

---

15. *Arabella*] a reference to Congreve's *Ode on Mrs. Arabella Hunt, Singing.*
  19. *Pastora*] a reference to Congreve's *The Mourning Muse of Alexis,* in which, under the name of Pastora, Congreve laments the death of Queen Mary.
  23. *William*] William III, eulogized by Congreve in *Pindarique Ode to the King, On His taking Namur.*

You check unjust esteem and fond desire,
And teach to scorn what else we should admire;   30
The just impression taught by you we bear,
The player acts the world, the world the player,
Whom still that world unjustly disesteems,
Though he alone professes what he seems.
But when your muse assumes her tragic part,   35
She conquers and she reigns in every heart;
To mourn with her men cheat their private woe,
And generous pity's all the grief they know.
The widow, who, impatient of delay,
From the town joys must mask it to the play,   40
Joins with your Mourning Bride's resistless moan,
And weeps a loss she slighted, when her own;
You give us torment, and you give us ease,
And vary our afflictions as you please,
Is not a heart so kind as yours in pain,   45
To load your friends with cares you only feign;
Your friends in grief, composed yourself, to leave?
But 'tis the only way you'll e'er deceive.
Then still, great sir, your moving power employ,
To lull our sorrow, and correct our joy.   50

R. STEELE

---

41. *Mourning Bride*] Congreve's sole tragedy, *The Mourning Bride* (1697).
51. *R. Steele*] Sir Richard Steele (1672–1729), essayist and dramatist.

TO THE RIGHT HONORABLE
RALPH, EARL OF MONTAGUE, &c.

MY LORD,

Whether the world will arraign me of vanity or not, that
I have presumed to dedicate this comedy to your Lordship,
I am yet in doubt, though it may be it is some degree of
vanity even to doubt of it. One who has at any time had   5
the honor of your Lordship's conversation, cannot be
supposed to think very meanly of that which he would prefer
to your perusal; yet it were to incur the imputation of too
much sufficiency, to pretend to such a merit as might abide
the test of your Lordship's censure.   10

Whatever value may be wanting to this play while yet it
is mine, will be sufficiently made up to it when it is once
become your Lordship's; and it is my security that I cannot
have overrated it more by my dedication than your Lordship will dignify it by your patronage.   15

That it succeeded on the stage was almost beyond my
expectation; for but little of it was prepared for that general
taste which seems now to be predominant in the palates of
our audience.

Those characters which are meant to be ridiculous in most   20
of our comedies are of fools so gross that, in my humble
opinion, they should rather disturb than divert the well-
natured and reflecting part of an audience; they are rather
objects of charity than contempt; and instead of moving our
mirth, they ought very often to excite our compassion.   25

This reflection moved me to design some characters which
should appear ridiculous, not so much through a natural
folly (which is incorrigible, and therefore not proper for
the stage) as through an affected wit; a wit, which, at the
same time that it is affected, is also false. As there is some 30
difficulty in the formation of a character of this nature, so

20. ridiculous] *Q1;* ridiculed *Q2,*
W1.

0.1. *Ralph, Earl of Montague*] Ralph Montagu (1638?–1709), created
Earl of Montagu in 1689 and Duke of Montagu in 1705.
7. *prefer*] offer.

–5–

there is some hazard which attends the progress of its
success upon the stage; for many come to a play so over-
charged with criticism that they very often let fly their
censure, when through their rashness they have mistaken   35
their aim. This I had occasion lately to observe; for this
play had been acted two or three days before some of these
hasty judges could find the leisure to distinguish betwixt the
character of a Witwoud and a Truewit.

I must beg your Lordship's pardon for this digression   40
from the true course of this epistle; but that it may not
seem altogether impertinent, I beg that I may plead the
occasion of it, in part of that excuse of which I stand in need,
for recommending this comedy to your protection. It is
only by the countenance of your Lordship, and the *few* so   45
qualified, that such who write with care and pains can hope
to be distinguished; for the prostituted name of *poet* promis-
cuously levels all that bear it.

Terence, the most correct writer in the world, had a
Scipio and a Laelius, if not to assist him, at least to support   50
him in his reputation; and notwithstanding his extraordinary merit, it may be their countenance was not more
than necessary.

The purity of his style, the delicacy of his turns, and the
justness of his characters were all of them beauties which the   55
greater part of his audience were incapable of tasting; some
of the coarsest strokes of Plautus, so severely censured by
Horace, were more likely to affect the multitude, such who
come with expectation to laugh out the last act of a play,
and are better entertained with two or three unseasonable   60
jests than with the artful solution of the *fable*.

As Terence excelled in his performances, so had he great
advantages to encourage his undertakings, for he built most
on the foundations of Menander; his plots were generally

---

39. *a Witwoud and a Truewit*] the would-be wit, Witwoud, in *The Way
of the World* and the genuinely witty Truewit in Jonson's *Epicoene; or The
Silent Woman* (1609).

49–50. *a Scipio and a Laelius*] Scipio Africanus and Caius Laelius,
patrons of the Roman comic dramatist Terence.

61. *fable*] plot.   64. *Menander*] Greek writer of New Comedy.

modeled, and his characters ready drawn to his hand. He 65
copied Menander, and Menander had no less light in the
formation of his characters from the observations of Theophrastus, of whom he was a disciple; and Theophrastus, it is
known, was not only the disciple, but the immediate successor of Aristotle, the first and greatest judge of poetry. These 70
were great models to design by; and the further advantage
which Terence possessed, towards giving his plays the due
ornaments of purity of style and justness of manners, was
not less considerable from the freedom of conversation which
was permitted him with Laelius and Scipio, two of the great- 75
est and most polite men of his age. And indeed the privilege
of such a conversation is the only certain means of attaining
to the perfection of dialogue.

If it has happened in any part of this comedy that I have
gained a turn of style or expression more correct, or at least 80
more corrigible, than in those which I have formerly
written, I must, with equal pride and gratitude, ascribe it
to the honor of your Lordship's admitting me into your
conversation, and that of a society where everybody else was
so well worthy of you, in your retirement last summer from 85
the town; for it was immediately after that this comedy was
written. If I have failed in my performance, it is only to be
regretted, where there were so many not inferior either to a
Scipio or a Laelius, that there should be one wanting equal
to the capacity of a Terence. 90

If I am not mistaken, poetry is almost the only art which
has not yet laid claim to your Lordship's patronage. Archi-
tecture and painting, to the great honor of our country,
have flourished under your influence and protection. In the
meantime, poetry, the eldest sister of all arts, and parent 95
of most, seems to have resigned her birthright, by having
neglected to pay her duty to your Lordship, and by permitting others of a later extraction to prepossess that place in
your esteem to which none can pretend a better title. Poetry,

90. to the capacity of] *Q1;* in
capacity to *W1.*

67–68. *Theophrastus*] Greek author, whose *Characters* had a marked
influence on the "character writing" of the seventeenth century.

in its nature, is sacred to the good and great; the relation 100
between them is reciprocal, and they are ever propitious to
it. It is the privilege of poetry to address to them, and it is
their prerogative alone to give it protection.

This received maxim is a general apology for all writers
who consecrate their labors to great men; but I could wish 105
at this time that this address were exempted from the
common pretense of all dedications; and that, as I can
distinguish your Lordship even among the most deserving, so
this offering might become remarkable by some particular
instance of respect, which should assure your Lordship that I 110
am, with all due sense of your extreme worthiness and
humanity,

My Lord,
Your Lordship's most obedient
and most obliged humble servant 115
WILL. CONGREVE

PROLOGUE

Spoken by Mr. Betterton

Of those few fools, who with ill stars are cursed,
Sure scribbling fools, called poets, fare the worst;
For they're a sort of fools which Fortune makes,
And after she has made 'em fools, forsakes.
With Nature's oafs 'tis quite a different case,   5
For Fortune favors all her idiot race;
In her own nest the cuckoo eggs we find,
O'er which she broods to hatch the changeling kind.
No portion for her own she has to spare,
So much she dotes on her adopted care.   10
    Poets are bubbles, by the town drawn in,
Suffered at first some trifling stakes to win;
But what unequal hazards do they run!
Each time they write they venture all they've won;
The squire that's buttered still is sure to be undone.   15
This author, heretofore, has found your favor,
But pleads no merit from his past behavior.
To build on that might prove a vain presumption,
Should grants to poets made admit resumption;
And in Parnassus he must lose his seat   20
If that be found a forfeited estate.
    He owns, with toil he wrote the following scenes,
But if they're naught ne'er spare him for his pains.
Damn him the more; have no commiseration
For dullness on mature deliberation.   25
He swears he'll not resent one hissed-off scene,
Nor, like those peevish wits, his play maintain,
Who, to assert their sense, your taste arraign.
Some plot we think he has, and some new thought,
Some humor too, no farce—but that's a fault.   30
Satire, he thinks, you ought not to expect;

---

5. *Nature's oafs*] Nature's stupid children.
7. *cuckoo eggs*] referring to the habit of cuckoos of laying eggs in the nests of other birds.
11. *bubbles*] dupes.   15. *buttered*] flattered.

For so reformed a town who dares correct?
To please this time has been his sole pretense;
He'll not instruct, lest it should give offense.
Should he by chance a knave or fool expose   35
That hurts none here; sure here are none of those.
In short, our play shall (with your leave to show it)
Give you one instance of a passive poet,
Who to your judgments yields all resignation;
So save or damn, after your own discretion.   40

DRAMATIS PERSONAE

Men

FAINALL, in love with MRS. MARWOOD	*Mr. Betterton*
MIRABELL, in love with MRS. MILLAMANT	*Mr. Verbruggen*
WITWOUD, Followers of MRS. MILLAMANT	*Mr. Bowen*
PETULANT,	*Mr. Bowman*
SIR WILFULL WITWOUD, Half-brother to WITWOUD, and Nephew to LADY WISHFORT	*Mr. Underhill*
WAITWELL, Servant to MIRABELL	*Mr. Bright*

Women

LADY WISHFORT, Enemy to MIRABELL, for having falsely pretended love to her	*Mrs. Leigh*
MRS. MILLAMANT, A fine Lady, Niece to LADY WISHFORT, and loves MIRABELL	*Mrs. Bracegirdle*
MRS. MARWOOD, Friend to MR. FAINALL, and likes MIRABELL	*Mrs. Barry*
MRS. FAINALL, Daughter to LADY WISHFORT, and Wife to FAINALL, formerly Friend to MIRABELL	*Mrs. Bowman*
FOIBLE, Woman to LADY WISHFORT	*Mrs. Willis*
MINCING, Woman to MRS. MILLAMANT	*Mrs. Prince*

Dancers, Footmen, and Attendants

SCENE—LONDON

The time equal to that of the presentation.

The Way of the World
A Comedy

[I]   *A Chocolate-house.*
Mirabell *and* Fainall, *rising from cards;* Betty *waiting.*

MIRABELL.

You are a fortunate man, Mr. Fainall.

FAINALL.

Have we done?

MIRABELL.

What you please. I'll play on to entertain you.

FAINALL.

No, I'll give you your revenge another time, when you are
not so indifferent; you are thinking of something else now,   5
and play too negligently. The coldness of a losing gamester
lessens the pleasure of the winner. I'd no more play with a
man that slighted his ill fortune than I'd make love to a
woman who undervalued the loss of her reputation.

MIRABELL.

You have a taste extremely delicate and are for refining on   10
your pleasures.

FAINALL.

Prithee, why so reserved? Something has put you out of
humor.

MIRABELL.

Not at all; I happen to be grave today, and you are gay;
that's all.   15

FAINALL.

Confess, Millamant and you quarreled last night, after I
left you; my fair cousin has some humors that would tempt

---

17. *humors*] moods.

the patience of a stoic. What, some coxcomb came in, and
was well received by her, while you were by.

MIRABELL.

Witwoud and Petulant, and what was worse, her aunt, your   20
wife's mother, my evil genius; or to sum up all in her own
name, my old Lady Wishfort came in.

FAINALL.

Oh, there it is then! She has a lasting passion for you, and
with reason. What, then my wife was there?

MIRABELL.

Yes, and Mrs. Marwood and three or four more, whom I   25
never saw before. Seeing me, they all put on their grave
faces, whispered one another; then complained aloud of the
vapors, and after fell into a profound silence.

FAINALL.

They had a mind to be rid of you.

MIRABELL.

For which reason I resolved not to stir. At last the good old   30
lady broke through her painful taciturnity, with an invective
against long visits. I would not have understood her, but
Millamant joining in the argument, I rose and with a con-
strained smile told her, I thought nothing was so easy as to
know when a visit began to be troublesome. She reddened   35
and I withdrew, without expecting her reply.

FAINALL.

You were to blame to resent what she spoke only in compliance with her aunt.

MIRABELL.

She is more mistress of herself than to be under the
necessity of such a resignation.   40

FAINALL.

What? though half her fortune depends upon her marrying
with my lady's approbation?

MIRABELL.

I was then in such a humor, that I should have been better
pleased if she had been less discreet.

---

28. *vapors*] a fashionable disorder indicating a depressed nervous condition.

FAINALL.

    Now I remember, I wonder not they were weary of you. 45
Last night was one of their cabal-nights; they have 'em three
times a week, and meet by turns, at one another's apart-
ments, where they come together like the coroner's inquest,
to sit upon the murdered reputations of the week. You and
I are excluded; and it was once proposed that all the male 50
sex should be excepted; but somebody moved that, to
avoid scandal, there might be one man of the community;
upon which motion Witwoud and Petulant were enrolled
members.

MIRABELL.

    And who may have been the foundress of this sect? My 55
Lady Wishfort, I warrant, who publishes her detestation
of mankind, and full of the vigor of fifty-five, declares for
a friend and ratafia; and let posterity shift for itself, she'll
breed no more.

FAINALL.

    The discovery of your sham addresses to her, to conceal 60
your love to her niece, has provoked this separation. Had
you dissembled better, things might have continued in the
state of nature.

MIRABELL.

    I did as much as man could, with any reasonable con-
science. I proceeded to the very last act of flattery with her, 65
and was guilty of a song in her commendation. Nay, I got
a friend to put her into a lampoon, and compliment her
with the imputation of an affair with a young fellow, which
I carried so far, that I told her the malicious town took
notice that she was grown fat of a sudden; and when she lay 70
in of a dropsy, persuaded her she was reported to be in
labor. The devil's in't, if an old woman is to be flattered
further, unless a man should endeavor downright personally
to debauch her; and that my virtue forbade me. But for the
discovery of that amour, I am indebted to your friend, or 75
your wife's friend, Mrs. Marwood.

75. that amour] *Q1;* this amour
Q2, W1.

---

   46. *cabal-nights*] private evening parties of a small group of intriguers.
   58. *ratafia*] a cordial flavored with certain fruits.

FAINALL.

What should provoke her to be your enemy, unless she has
made you advances, which you have slighted? Women do
not easily forgive omissions of that nature.

MIRABELL.

She was always civil to me, till of late. I confess I am not   80
one of those coxcombs who are apt to interpret a woman's
good manners to her prejudice, and think that she who does
not refuse 'em everything can refuse 'em nothing.

FAINALL.

You are a gallant man, Mirabell; and though you may
have cruelty enough not to satisfy a lady's longing, you have   85
too much generosity not to be tender of her honor. Yet you
speak with an indifference which seems to be affected, and
confesses you are conscious of a negligence.

MIRABELL.

You pursue the argument with a distrust that seems to be
unaffected, and confesses you are conscious of a concern for   90
which the lady is more indebted to you than your wife.

FAINALL.

Fie, fie, friend! If you grow censorious, I must leave you.
I'll look upon the gamesters in the next room.

MIRABELL.

Who are they?

FAINALL.

Petulant and Witwoud. [*To Betty.*] Bring me some   95
chocolate.   *Exit.*

MIRABELL.

Betty, what says your clock?

BETTY.

Turned of the last canonical hour, sir.   *Exit.*

MIRABELL.

How pertinently the jade answers me! (*Looking on his
watch.*) Ha? almost one o'clock! Oh, y'are come!   100

---

77. unless] *W1*; without *Q1–2*.   99. answers me] *Q1, W1;* answers
                                         we *Q2.*

---

98. *last canonical hour*] twelve o'clock (noon). At this date the canonical
hours, when marriages might be legally performed, were from eight to
twelve in the morning.

Enter a Servant.

Well, is the grand affair over? You have been something
tedious.

SERVANT.

Sir, there's such coupling at Pancras, that they stand behind
one another, as 'twere in a country dance. Ours was the
last couple to lead up; and no hopes appearing of dispatch, 105
besides the parson growing hoarse, we were afraid his lungs
would have failed before it came to our turn; so we drove
round to Duke's Place, and there they were riveted in a
trice.

MIRABELL.

So, so, you are sure they are married.   110

SERVANT.

Married and bedded, sir; I am witness.

MIRABELL.

Have you the certificate?

SERVANT.

Here it is, sir.

MIRABELL.

Has the tailor brought Waitwell's clothes home, and the
new liveries?   115

SERVANT.

Yes, sir.

MIRABELL.

That's well. Do you go home again, d'ye hear, and adjourn
the consummation till farther order; bid Waitwell shake his
ears, and Dame Partlet rustle up her feathers, and meet me at
one o'clock by Rosamond's Pond, that I may see her before 120

117. d'ye hear] *Q2, W1;* d'ee *Q1.   followed throughout the text.*
The d'ye *of Q2 and W1 has been*

---

103. *Pancras*] St. Pancras Church, where couples might marry without
licenses.
108. *Duke's Place*] St. James' Church in Aldgate, where marriages,
sometimes referred to as Fleet weddings, could also be performed without
licenses.
119. *Partlet*] Pertelote, wife of Chauntecleer in Chaucer's *The Nun's
Priest's Tale.*
120. *Rosamond's Pond*] a little lake in the southwest corner of St. James's
Park, around which Charles II planted groves, a resort of lovers.

she returns to her lady; and as you tender your ears, be
secret.   *Exit* Servant.

Re-enter Fainall [*and* Betty].

FAINALL.

Joy of your success, Mirabell; you look pleased.

MIRABELL.

Aye, I have been engaged in a matter of some sort of mirth,
which is not yet ripe for discovery. I am glad this is not a 125
cabal-night. I wonder, Fainall, that you who are married,
and of consequence should be discreet, will suffer your wife
to be of such a party.

FAINALL.

Faith, I am not jealous. Besides, most who are engaged are
women and relations; and for the men, they are of a kind 130
too contemptible to give scandal.

MIRABELL.

I am of another opinion. The greater the coxcomb, always
the more scandal; for a woman who is not a fool can have
but one reason for associating with a man that is.

FAINALL.

Are you jealous as often as you see Witwoud entertained by 135
Millamant?

MIRABELL.

Of her understanding I am, if not of her person.

FAINALL.

You do her wrong; for, to give her her due, she has wit.

MIRABELL.

She has beauty enough to make any man think so, and complaisance enough not to contradict him who shall tell her so. 140

FAINALL.

For a passionate lover, methinks you are a man somewhat
too discerning in the failings of your mistress.

MIRABELL.

And for a discerning man, somewhat too passionate a lover;
for I like her with all her faults; nay, like her for her faults.
Her follies are so natural, or so artful, that they become her; 145

---

121. *tender*] have regard for.

and those affectations which in another woman would be
odious, serve but to make her more agreeable. I'll tell thee,
Fainall, she once used me with that insolence, that in
revenge I took her to pieces; sifted her and separated her
failings; I studied 'em, and got 'em by rote. The catalogue 150
was so large that I was not without hopes one day or other
to hate her heartily: to which end I so used myself to think
of 'em that at length, contrary to my design and expectation,
they gave me every hour less and less disturbance; till in a
few days it became habitual to me to remember 'em without 155
being displeased. They are now grown as familiar to me as
my own frailties; and in all probability, in a little time
longer I shall like 'em as well.

FAINALL.

Marry her, marry her! Be half as well acquainted with
her charms as you are with her defects, and my life on't, you 160
are your own man again.

MIRABELL.

Say you so?

FAINALL.

Aye, aye, I have experience: I have a wife, and so forth.

Enter Messenger.

MESSENGER.

Is one Squire Witwoud here?

BETTY.

Yes; what's your business?   165

MESSENGER.

I have a letter for him, from his brother Sir Wilfull, which
I am charged to deliver into his own hands.

BETTY.

He's in the next room, friend; that way.   *Exit* Messenger

MIRABELL.

What, is the chief of that noble family in town, Sir Wilfull
Witwoud?   170

FAINALL.

He is expected today. Do you know him?

---

149. *sifted*] examined very closely.
152. *used*] accustomed.

MIRABELL.

I have seen him. He promises to be an extraordinary
person; I think you have the honor to be related to him.

FAINALL.

Yes, he is half brother to this Witwoud by a former wife,
who was sister to my Lady Wishfort, my wife's mother. If 175
you marry Millamant, you must call cousins too.

MIRABELL.

I had rather be his relation than his acquaintance.

FAINALL.

He comes to town in order to equip himself for travel.

MIRABELL.

For travel! Why the man I mean is above forty.

FAINALL.

No matter for that; 'tis for the honor of England that all 180
Europe should know we have blockheads of all ages.

MIRABELL.

I wonder there is not an act of parliament to save the
credit of the nation, and prohibit the exportation of fools.

FAINALL.

By no means; 'tis better as 'tis. 'Tis better to trade with a
little loss, than to be quite eaten up with being over- 185
stocked.

MIRABELL.

Pray, are the follies of this knight-errant and those of the
squire his brother anything related?

FAINALL.

Not at all; Witwoud grows by the knight, like a medlar
grafted on a crab. One will melt in your mouth, and t'other 190
set your teeth on edge; one is all pulp, and the other all core.

MIRABELL.

So one will be rotten before he be ripe, and the other will be
rotten without ever being ripe at all.

FAINALL.

Sir Wilfull is an odd mixture of bashfulness and obstinacy.

189–190. *a medlar grafted on a crab*] a soft pulpy fruit grafted on a crab-
apple.

But when he's drunk, he's as loving as the monster in *The* 195
Tempest, and much after the same manner. To give t'other
his due, he has something of good nature and does not always
want wit.

MIRABELL.

Not always; but as often as his memory fails him, and his
commonplace of comparisons. He is a fool with a good 200
memory and some few scraps of other folks' wit. He is one
whose conversation can never be approved, yet it is now
and then to be endured. He has indeed one good quality, he
is not exceptious; for he so passionately affects the reputation
of understanding raillery, that he will construe an affront 205
into a jest, and call downright rudeness and ill language
satire and fire.

FAINALL.

If you have a mind to finish his picture, you have an opportunity to do it at full length. Behold the original!

Enter Witwoud.

WITWOUD.

Afford me your compassion, my dears! Pity me, Fainall! 210
Mirabell, pity me!

MIRABELL.

I do from my soul.

FAINALL.

Why, what's the matter?

WITWOUD.

No letters for me, Betty?

BETTY.

Did not the messenger bring you one but now, sir?   215

---

196. t'other] *W1;* the t'other *Q1.*   215. the messenger] *Q1;* a messen-
                                                              ger *W1.*

195–196. *the monster in The Tempest*] In Dryden and D'Avenant's *The
Tempest* (1667), Trincalo says of Caliban: "The poor monster is loving in
his drink." In the same play Sycorax, Caliban's sister, is also a loving
monster, but without the incentive of wine.

198. *want*] lack.

200. *commonplace of comparisons*] commonplace, or memorandum, book
in which he records clever remarks which he has heard or read.

204. *is not exceptious*] does not contradict.

WITWOUD.

Aye, but no other?

BETTY.

No, sir.

WITWOUD.

That's hard, that's very hard. A messenger, a mule, a beast
of burden! He has brought me a letter from the fool my
brother, as heavy as a panegyric in a funeral sermon, or a 220
copy of commendatory verses from one poet to another.
And what's worse, 'tis as sure a forerunner of the author as
an epistle dedicatory.

MIRABELL.

A fool, and your brother Witwoud!

WITWOUD.

Aye, aye, my half brother. My half brother he is, no nearer 225
upon honor.

MIRABELL.

Then 'tis possible he may be but half a fool.

WITWOUD.

Good, good, Mirabell, *le drôle!* Good, good; hang him,
don't let's talk of him. Fainall, how does your lady? Gad, I
say anything in the world to get this fellow out of my head. 230
I beg pardon that I should ask a man of pleasure, and the
town, a question at once so foreign and domestic. But I talk
like an old maid at a marriage, I don't know what I say; but
she's the best woman in the world.

FAINALL.

'Tis well you don't know what you say, or else your 235
commendation would go near to make me either vain or
jealous.

WITWOUD.

No man in town lives well with a wife but Fainall. Your
judgment, Mirabell.

MIRABELL.

You had better step and ask his wife, if you would be 240
credibly informed.

WITWOUD.

Mirabell.

---

228. *le drôle*] the amusing fellow.

MIRABELL.

Aye.

WITWOUD.

My dear, I ask ten thousand pardons. Gad, I have forgot
what I was going to say to you!   245

MIRABELL.

I thank you heartily, heartily.

WITWOUD.

No, but prithee excuse me: my memory is such a memory.

MIRABELL.

Have a care of such apologies, Witwoud; for I never knew
a fool but he affected to complain, either of the spleen or his
memory.   250

FAINALL.

What have you done with Petulant?

WITWOUD.

He's reckoning his money, my money it was. I have no
luck today.

FAINALL.

You may allow him to win of you at play, for you are sure
to be too hard for him at repartee; since you monopolize the 255
wit that is between you, the fortune must be his of course.

MIRABELL.

I don't find that Petulant confesses the superiority of wit
to be your talent, Witwoud.

WITWOUD.

Come, come, you are malicious now, and would breed
debates. Petulant's my friend, and a very honest fellow, and 260
a very pretty fellow, and has a smattering—faith and troth,
a pretty deal of an odd sort of a small wit: nay, I'll do him
justice. I'm his friend, I won't wrong him neither. And if
he had but any judgment in the world, he would not be
altogether contemptible. Come, come, don't detract from 265
the merits of my friend.

FAINALL.

You don't take your friend to be over-nicely bred?

263. neither] *Q1; omitted in W1.*   264. but] *Q1; omitted in W1.*

249. *spleen*] low spirits believed to result from a diseased condition of
that organ.

WITWOUD.

No, no, hang him, the rogue has no manners at all, that
I must own. No more breeding than a bum-baily, that I
grant you. 'Tis pity, faith; the fellow has fire and life.   270

MIRABELL.

What, courage?

WITWOUD.

Hum, faith, I don't know as to that, I can't say as to that.
Yes, faith, in a controversy he'll contradict anybody.

MIRABELL.

Though 'twere a man whom he feared, or a woman whom
he loved.   275

WITWOUD.

Well, well, he does not always think before he speaks; we
have all our failings. You're too hard upon him, you are,
faith. Let me excuse him. I can defend most of his faults,
except one or two. One he has, that's the truth on't; if he
were my brother, I could not acquit him. That, indeed, I   280
could wish were otherwise.

MIRABELL.

Aye, marry, what's that, Witwoud?

WITWOUD.

Oh, pardon me! Expose the infirmities of my friend! No, my
dear, excuse me there.

FAINALL.

What, I warrant he's unsincere, or 'tis some such trifle.   285

WITWOUD.

No, no, what if he be? 'Tis no matter for that, his wit will
excuse that. A wit should no more be sincere than a
woman constant; one argues a decay of parts, as t'other of
beauty.

MIRABELL.

Maybe you think him too positive?   290

WITWOUD.

No, no, his being positive is an incentive to argument, and
keeps up conversation.

---

269. *bum-baily*] a low type of bailiff or sheriff's officer.
288. *parts*] talents.

FAINALL.

Too illiterate?

WITWOUD.

That! that's his happiness; his want of learning gives him
the more opportunities to show his natural parts.   295

MIRABELL.

He wants words?

WITWOUD.

Aye, but I like him for that now; for his want of words
gives me the pleasure very often to explain his meaning.

FAINALL.

He's impudent?

WITWOUD.

No, that's not it.   300

MIRABELL.

Vain?

WITWOUD.

No.

MIRABELL.

What! he speaks unseasonable truths sometimes, because he
has not wit enough to invent an evasion?

WITWOUD.

Truths! ha! ha! ha! No, no, since you will have it, I mean he   305
never speaks truth at all, that's all. He will lie like a chambermaid, or a woman of quality's porter. Now that is a fault.

Enter Coachman.

COACHMAN.

Is Master Petulant here, mistress?

BETTY.

Yes.

COACHMAN.

Three gentlewomen in the coach would speak with him.   310

FAINALL.

Oh brave Petulant! Three!

BETTY.

I'll tell him.

310. the coach] *Q1;* a coach *W1.*

COACHMAN.

> You must bring two dishes of chocolate and a glass of
> cinnamon-water.   [*Exeunt* Betty *and* Coachman.]

WITWOUD.

> That should be for two fasting strumpets, and a bawd 315
> troubled with wind. Now you may know what the three
> are.

MIRABELL.

> You are very free with your friend's acquaintance.

WITWOUD.

> Aye, aye, friendship without freedom is as dull as love
> without enjoyment, or wine without toasting; but to tell 320
> you a secret, these are trulls that he allows coach-hire,
> and something more, by the week, to call on him once a day
> at public places.

MIRABELL.

> How!

WITWOUD.

> You shall see he won't go to 'em because there's no more 325
> company here to take notice of him. Why, this is nothing to
> what he used to do: before he found out this way, I have
> known him call for himself.

FAINALL.

> Call for himself? What dost thou mean?

WITWOUD.

> Mean! Why, he would slip you out of this chocolate-house, 330
> just when you had been talking to him. As soon as your
> back was turned, whip, he was gone! Then trip to his lodg-
> ing, clap on a hood and scarf, and mask, slap into a hackney-
> coach, and drive hither to the door again in a trice, where
> he would send in for himself; that I mean, call for himself, 335
> wait for himself; nay, and what's more, not finding himself,
> sometimes leave a letter for himself.

MIRABELL.

> I confess this is something extraordinary. I believe he waits
> for himself now, he is so long a-coming. Oh! I ask his pardon.

---

314. *cinnamon-water*] a drink composed of sugar, spirits, powdered
cinnamon, and hot water, considered an aid to digestion.
321. *trulls*] prostitutes.

Enter Petulant [*and* Betty].

BETTY.

    Sir, the coach stays.   340

PETULANT.

    Well, well; I come. 'Sbud, a man had as good be a professed midwife as a professed whoremaster, at this rate! To be knocked up and raised at all hours, and in all places! Pox on 'em, I won't come! D'ye hear, tell 'em I won't come. Let 'em snivel and cry their hearts out.   345

FAINALL.

    You are very cruel, Petulant.

PETULANT.

    All's one, let it pass. I have a humor to be cruel.

MIRABELL.

    I hope they are not persons of condition that you use at this rate.

PETULANT.

    Condition! Condition's a dried fig, if I am not in humor! 350 By this hand, if they were your—a—a—your what-d'ye-call-'ems themselves, they must wait or rub off, if I want appetite.

MIRABELL.

    What-d'ye-call-'ems! What are they, Witwoud?

WITWOUD.

    Empresses, my dear; by your what-d'ye-call-'ems he means 355 sultana queens.

PETULANT.

    Aye, Roxolanas.

MIRABELL.

    Cry you mercy.

FAINALL.

    Witwoud says they are—

PETULANT.

    What does he say th'are?   360

---

341. *'Sbud*] a contraction of the oath *God's blood*.

352. *rub off*] clear out.

357. *Roxolanas*] Roxolana is the wife of Solyman the Magnificent in D'Avenant's *The Siege of Rhodes* (Part I, 1656, Part II, 1661).

WITWOUD.

I? Fine ladies, I say.

PETULANT.

Pass on, Witwoud. Harkee, by this light his relations: two co-heiresses his cousins, and an old aunt, that loves cater-wauling better than a conventicle.

WITWOUD.

Ha! ha! ha! I had a mind to see how the rogue would 365 come off. Ha! ha! ha! Gad, I can't be angry with him, if he had said they were my mother and my sisters.

MIRABELL.

No!

WITWOUD.

No; the rogue's wit and readiness of invention charm me. Dear Petulant! 370

BETTY.

They are gone, sir, in great anger.

PETULANT.

Enough, let 'em trundle. Anger helps complexion, saves paint.

FAINALL.

This continence is all dissembled; this is in order to have something to brag of the next time he makes court to 375 Millamant, and swear he has abandoned the whole sex for her sake.

MIRABELL.

Have you not left off your impudent pretensions there yet? I shall cut your throat some time or other, Petulant, about that business. 380

PETULANT.

Aye, aye, let that pass. There are other throats to be cut.

MIRABELL.

Meaning mine, sir?

PETULANT.

Not I. I mean nobody; I know nothing. But there are uncles and nephews in the world, and they may be rivals. What then? All's one for that. 385

---

362. *Harkee*] a corruption of *hark ye*.
364. *conventicle*] meetinghouse of a nonconformist sect.
372. *trundle*] roll along.

MIRABELL.

How! Harkee Petulant, come hither. Explain, or I shall call your interpreter.

PETULANT.

Explain! I know nothing. Why, you have an uncle, have you not, lately come to town, and lodges by my Lady Wishfort's?

MIRABELL.

True.   390

PETULANT.

Why, that's enough. You and he are not friends; and if he should marry and have a child, you may be disinherited, ha?

MIRABELL.

Where hast thou stumbled upon all this truth?

PETULANT.

All's one for that; why, then say I know something.   395

MIRABELL.

Come, thou art an honest fellow, Petulant, and shalt make love to my mistress, thou sha't, faith. What hast thou heard of my uncle?

PETULANT.

I? Nothing I. If throats are to be cut, let swords clash! Snug's the word; I shrug and am silent.   400

MIRABELL.

Oh, raillery, raillery! Come, I know thou art in the women's secrets. What, you're a cabalist; I know you stayed at Millamant's last night, after I went. Was there any mention made of my uncle or me? Tell me. If thou hadst but good nature equal to thy wit, Petulant, Tony Witwoud, 405 who is now thy competitor in fame, would show as dim by thee as a dead whiting's eye by a pearl of orient; he would no more be seen by thee than Mercury is by the sun. Come, I'm sure thou wo't tell me.

---

387. *your interpreter*] Witwoud (?).
400. *Snug's the word*] Secrecy's the watchword.
402. *cabalist*] secret intriguer.
408. *by thee*] beside thee.

PETULANT.

If I do, will you grant me common sense then for the 410
future?

MIRABELL.

Faith, I'll do what I can for thee; and I'll pray that Heaven
may grant it thee in the meantime.

PETULANT.

Well, harkee.   [Mirabell *and* Petulant *talk apart.*]

FAINALL.

Petulant and you both will find Mirabell as warm a rival as 415
a lover.

WITWOUD.

Pshaw! pshaw! That she laughs at Petulant is plain. And for
my part, but that it is almost a fashion to admire her, I
should—harkee, to tell you a secret, but let it go no further;
between friends, I shall never break my heart for her.   420

FAINALL.

How!

WITWOUD.

She's handsome; but she's a sort of an uncertain woman.

FAINALL.

I thought you had died for her.

WITWOUD.

Umh—no—

FAINALL.

She has wit.   425

WITWOUD.

'Tis what she will hardly allow anybody else. Now, demme,
I should hate that, if she were as handsome as Cleopatra.
Mirabell is not so sure of her as he thinks for.

FAINALL.

Why do you think so?

WITWOUD.

We stayed pretty late there last night, and heard something 430
of an uncle to Mirabell, who is lately come to town, and
is between him and the best part of his estate. Mirabell and
he are at some distance, as my Lady Wishfort has been told;

426. *demme*] damn me.

and you know she hates Mirabell worse than a Quaker hates
a parrot, or than a fishmonger hates a hard frost. Whether 435
this uncle has seen Mrs. Millamant or not, I cannot say;
but there were items of such a treaty being in embryo, and
if it should come to life, poor Mirabell would be in some
sort unfortunately fobbed, i'faith.

FAINALL.

'Tis impossible Millamant should hearken to it.   440

WITWOUD.

Faith, my dear, I can't tell; she's a woman and a kind of a
humorist.

MIRABELL.

And is this the sum of what you could collect last night?

PETULANT.

The quintessence. Maybe Witwoud knows more; he stayed
longer. Besides, they never mind him; they say anything 445
before him.

MIRABELL.

I thought you had been the greatest favorite.

PETULANT.

Aye, *tête à tête*, but not in public, because I make remarks.

MIRABELL.

You do?

PETULANT.

Aye, aye, pox, I'm malicious, man! Now he's soft, you 450
know, they are not in awe of him. The fellow's well-bred,
he's what you call a—what-d'ye-call-'em, a fine gentleman,
but he's silly withal.

MIRABELL.

I thank you. I know as much as my curiosity requires.
Fainall, are you for the Mall?   455

---

448. *tête à tête*] Spelled *tete a tete W1*;
teste a teste Q 1–2.

434–435. *worse than a Quaker hates a parrot*] i.e., because the parrot is so
talkative.
435. *or than a fishmonger hates a hard frost*] i.e., because cold weather
makes his work difficult.
439. *fobbed*] tricked.   442. *humorist*] one given to whims.
455. *the Mall*] a fashionable promenade adjoining St. James's Park,
now the street known as Pall Mall.

FAINALL.

Aye, I'll take a turn before dinner.

WITWOUD.

Aye, we'll all walk in the park; the ladies talked of being there.

MIRABELL.

I thought you were obliged to watch for your brother Sir Wilfull's arrival.   460

WITWOUD.

No, no, he comes to his aunt's, my Lady Wishfort. Pox on him! I shall be troubled with him too; what shall I do with the fool?

PETULANT.

Beg him for his estate, that I may beg you afterwards; and so have but one trouble with you both.   465

WITWOUD.

Oh, rare Petulant! Thou art as quick as a fire in a frosty morning; thou shalt to the Mall with us, and we'll be very severe.

PETULANT.

Enough, I'm in a humor to be severe.

MIRABELL.

Are you? Pray then walk by yourselves. Let not us be 470 accessory to your putting the ladies out of countenance with your senseless ribaldry, which you roar out aloud as often as they pass by you; and when you have made a handsome woman blush, then you think you have been severe.

PETULANT.

What, what? Then let 'em show their innocence by not 475 understanding what they hear, or else show their discretion by not hearing what they would not be thought to understand.

MIRABELL.

But hast not thou then sense enough to know that thou ought'st to be most ashamed thyself, when thou hast put 480 another out of countenance?

PETULANT.

Not I, by this hand! I always take blushing either for a sign of guilt or ill-breeding.

MIRABELL.

I confess you ought to think so. You are in the right, that
you may plead the error of your judgment in defense of your 485
practice.

Where modesty's ill manners, 'tis but fit
That impudence and malice pass for wit.   *Exeunt.*

[II]   *St. James's Park.*
                Enter Mrs. Fainall *and* Mrs. Marwood.

MRS. FAINALL.

Aye, aye, dear Marwood, if we will be happy, we must
find the means in ourselves, and among ourselves. Men
are ever in extremes, either doting or averse. While they are
lovers, if they have fire and sense, their jealousies are insupportable. And when they cease to love (we ought to   5
think at least) they loathe; they look upon us with horror
and distaste; they meet us like the ghosts of what we were,
and as such, fly from us.

MRS. MARWOOD.

True, 'tis an unhappy circumstance of life, that love should
ever die before us; and that the man so often should outlive   10
the lover. But say what you will, 'tis better to be left than
never to have been loved. To pass our youth in dull indifference, to refuse the sweets of life because they once must leave
us, is as preposterous as to wish to have been born old,
because we one day must be old. For my part, my youth   15
may wear and waste, but it shall never rust in my possession.

MRS. FAINALL.

Then it seems you dissemble an aversion to mankind, only
in compliance with my mother's humor.

MRS. MARWOOD.

Certainly. To be free, I have no taste of those insipid dry
discourses with which our sex of force must entertain them-   20
selves, apart from men. We may affect endearments to each
other, profess eternal friendships, and seem to dote like

18. compliance with] *Q1;* compliance to *W1.*
_____

19. *free*] frank.

lovers; but 'tis not in our natures long to persevere. Love will
resume his empire in our breasts; and every heart, or soon or
late, receive and readmit him as its lawful tyrant.   25

MRS. FAINALL.

Bless me, how have I been deceived! Why you profess a
libertine!

MRS. MARWOOD.

You see my friendship by my freedom. Come, be as sincere,
acknowledge that your sentiments agree with mine.

MRS. FAINALL.

Never!   30

MRS. MARWOOD.

You hate mankind?

MRS. FAINALL.

Heartily, inveterately.

MRS. MARWOOD.

Your husband?

MRS. FAINALL.

Most transcendently; aye, though I say it, meritoriously.

MRS. MARWOOD.

Give me your hand upon it.   35

MRS. FAINALL.

There.

MRS. MARWOOD.

I join with you; what I have said has been to try you.

MRS. FAINALL.

Is it possible? Dost thou hate those vipers, men?

MRS. MARWOOD.

I have done hating 'em, and am now come to despise 'em;
the next thing I have to do, is eternally to forget 'em.   40

MRS. FAINALL.

There spoke the spirit of an Amazon, a Penthesilea.

MRS. MARWOOD.

And yet I am thinking sometimes to carry my aversion
further.

---

34. *transcendently*] supremely.
41. *Penthesilea*] famous Queen of the Amazons, a race of female
warriors.

MRS. FAINALL.

How?

MRS. MARWOOD.

Faith, by marrying; if I could but find one that loved me   45
very well and would be thoroughly sensible of ill usage, I
think I should do myself the violence of undergoing the
ceremony.

MRS. FAINALL.

You would not make him a cuckold?

MRS. MARWOOD.

No, but I'd make him believe I did, and that's as bad.   50

MRS. FAINALL.

Why had not you as good do it?

MRS. MARWOOD.

Oh, if he should ever discover it, he would then know the
worst, and be out of his pain; but I would have him ever to
continue upon the rack of fear and jealousy.

MRS. FAINALL.

Ingenious mischief! Would thou wert married to Mirabell.   55

MRS. MARWOOD.

Would I were!

MRS. FAINALL.

You change color.

MRS. MARWOOD.

Because I hate him.

MRS. FAINALL.

So do I; but I can hear him named. But what reason have
you to hate him in particular?   60

MRS. MARWOOD.

I never loved him; he is, and always was, insufferably
proud.

MRS. FAINALL.

By the reason you give for your aversion, one would think it
dissembled; for you have laid a fault to his charge of which his
enemies must acquit him.   65

MRS. MARWOOD.

Oh, then it seems you are one of his favorable enemies!
Methinks you look a little pale, and now you flush again.

MRS. FAINALL.

Do I? I think I am a little sick o' the sudden.

MRS. MARWOOD.

What ails you?

MRS. FAINALL.

My husband. Don't you see him? He turned short upon me   70
unawares, and has almost overcome me.

Enter Fainall *and* Mirabell.

MRS. MARWOOD.

Ha! ha! ha! He comes opportunely for you.

MRS. FAINALL.

For you, for he has brought Mirabell with him.

FAINALL.

My dear!

MRS. FAINALL.

My soul!   75

FAINALL.

You don't look well today, child.

MRS. FAINALL.

D'ye think so?

MIRABELL.

He is the only man that does, madam.

MRS. FAINALL.

The only man that would tell me so at least; and the only
man from whom I could hear it without mortification.   80

FAINALL.

Oh my dear, I am satisfied of your tenderness; I know you
cannot resent anything from me, especially what is an effect
of my concern.

MRS. FAINALL.

Mr. Mirabell, my mother interrupted you in a pleasant
relation last night; I would fain hear it out.   85

MIRABELL.

The persons concerned in that affair have yet a tolerable
reputation. I am afraid Mr. Fainall will be censorious.

MRS. FAINALL.

He has a humor more prevailing than his curiosity, and
will willingly dispense with the hearing of one scandalous
story, to avoid giving an occasion to make another by   90
being seen to walk with his wife. This way, Mr. Mirabell,
and I dare promise you will oblige us both.

Exeunt Mrs. Fainall *and* Mirabell.

FAINALL.

Excellent creature! Well, sure if I should live to be rid of my wife, I should be a miserable man.

MRS. MARWOOD.

Aye!   95

FAINALL.

For having only that one hope, the accomplishment of it, of consequence must put an end to all my hopes; and what a wretch is he who must survive his hopes! Nothing remains when that day comes, but to sit down and weep like Alexander, when he wanted other worlds to conquer.   100

MRS. MARWOOD.

Will you not follow 'em?

FAINALL.

Faith, I think not.

MRS. MARWOOD.

Pray let us; I have a reason.

FAINALL.

You are not jealous?

MRS. MARWOOD.

Of whom?   105

FAINALL.

Of Mirabell.

MRS. MARWOOD.

If I am, is it inconsistent with my love to you that I am tender of your honor?

FAINALL.

You would intimate then, as if there were a fellow-feeling between my wife and him.   110

MRS. MARWOOD.

I think she does not hate him to that degree she would be thought.

FAINALL.

But he, I fear, is too insensible.

MRS. MARWOOD.

It may be you are deceived.

99–100. *Alexander*] Alexander the Great, King of Macedon.

FAINALL.

It may be so. I do now begin to apprehend it. 115

MRS. MARWOOD.

What?

FAINALL.

That I have been deceived, madam, and you are false.

MRS. MARWOOD.

That I am false! What mean you?

FAINALL.

To let you know I see through all your little arts. Come,
you both love him; and both have equally dissembled your 120
aversion. Your mutual jealousies of one another have made
you clash till you have both struck fire. I have seen the warm
confession reddening on your cheeks, and sparkling from
your eyes.

MRS. MARWOOD.

You do me wrong. 125

FAINALL.

I do not. 'Twas for my ease to oversee and wilfully neglect
the gross advances made him by my wife; that by permitting
her to be engaged, I might continue unsuspected in my
pleasures, and take you oftener to my arms in full security.
But could you think, because the nodding husband would 130
not wake, that e'er the watchful lover slept?

MRS. MARWOOD.

And wherewithal can you reproach me?

FAINALL.

With infidelity, with loving of another, with love of Mirabell.

MRS. MARWOOD.

'Tis false. I challenge you to show an instance that can
confirm your groundless accusation. I hate him. 135

FAINALL.

And wherefore do you hate him? He is insensible, and your
resentment follows his neglect. An instance? The injuries
you have done him are a proof, your interposing in his love.
What cause had you to make discoveries of his pretended

115. I do now] *Q1;* I do not now
Q2, W1.

126. *oversee*] overlook.

-37-

passion? To undeceive the credulous aunt, and be the 140
officious obstacle of his match with Millamant?

MRS. MARWOOD.

My obligations to my lady urged me; I had professed a
friendship to her, and could not see her easy nature so
abused by that dissembler.

FAINALL.

What, was it conscience then? Professed a friendship! Oh, 145
the pious friendships of the female sex!

MRS. MARWOOD.

More tender, more sincere, and more enduring, than all
the vain and empty vows of men, whether professing love
to us, or mutual faith to one another.

FAINALL.

Ha! ha! ha! you are my wife's friend too.   150

MRS. MARWOOD.

Shame and ingratitude! Do you reproach me? You, you
upbraid me! Have I been false to her, through strict
fidelity to you, and sacrificed my friendship to keep my love
inviolate? And have you the baseness to charge me with the
guilt, unmindful of the merit! To you it should be merito- 155
rious, that I have been vicious; and do you reflect that
guilt upon me, which should lie buried in your bosom?

FAINALL.

You misinterpret my reproof. I meant but to remind you of
the slight account you once could make of strictest ties, when
set in comparison with your love to me.   160

MRS. MARWOOD.

'Tis false; you urged it with deliberate malice! 'Twas spoke
in scorn, and I never will forgive it.

FAINALL.

Your guilt, not your resentment, begets your rage. If yet you
loved, you could forgive a jealousy; but you are stung to find
you are discovered.   165

MRS. MARWOOD.

It shall be all discovered. You too shall be discovered; be
sure you shall. I can but be exposed. If I do it myself, I
shall prevent your baseness.

---

168. *prevent*] anticipate.

FAINALL.

Why, what will you do?

MRS. MARWOOD.

Disclose it to your wife; own what has passed between us. 170

FAINALL.

Frenzy!

MRS. MARWOOD.

By all my wrongs I'll do't! I'll publish to the world the
injuries you have done me, both in my fame and fortune!
With both I trusted you, you bankrupt in honor, as indigent
of wealth.   175

FAINALL.

Your fame I have preserved. Your fortune has been be-
stowed as the prodigality of your love would have it, in
pleasures which we both have shared. Yet had not you been
false, I had ere this repaid it. 'Tis true, had you permitted
Mirabell with Millamant to have stolen their marriage, my 180
lady had been incensed beyond all means of reconcilement;
Millamant had forfeited the moiety of her fortune, which
then would have descended to my wife. And wherefore did
I marry, but to make lawful prize of a rich widow's wealth,
and squander it on love and you?   185

MRS. MARWOOD.

Deceit and frivolous pretense!

FAINALL.

Death, am I not married? What's pretense? Am I not
imprisoned, fettered? Have I not a wife? Nay a wife that
was a widow, a young widow, a handsome widow; and
would be again a widow, but that I have a heart of proof, 190
and something of a constitution to bustle through the ways of
wedlock and this world. Will you yet be reconciled to truth
and me?

MRS. MARWOOD.

Impossible. Truth and you are inconsistent. I hate you, and
shall for ever.   195

FAINALL.

For loving you?

---

182. *moiety*] half.
190. *of proof*] of tested strength.

MRS. MARWOOD.

I loathe the name of love after such usage; and next to the
guilt with which you would asperse me, I scorn you most.
Farewell!

FAINALL.

Nay, we must not part thus.   200

MRS. MARWOOD.

Let me go.

FAINALL.

Come, I'm sorry.

MRS. MARWOOD.

I care not, let me go. Break my hands, do! I'd leave 'em
to get loose.

FAINALL.

I would not hurt you for the world. Have I no other hold to 205
keep you here?

MRS. MARWOOD.

Well, I have deserved it all.

FAINALL.

You know I love you.

MRS. MARWOOD.

Poor dissembling! Oh, that—Well, it is not yet—

FAINALL.

What? what is it not? What is it not yet? It is not yet too 210
late—

MRS. MARWOOD.

No, it is not yet too late; I have that comfort.

FAINALL.

It is, to love another.

MRS. MARWOOD.

But not to loathe, detest, abhor mankind, myself, and the
whole treacherous world.   215

FAINALL.

Nay, this is extravagance. Come, I ask your pardon. No
tears. I was to blame; I could not love you and be easy in
my doubts. Pray, forbear. I believe you. I'm convinced I've
done you wrong; and any way, every way will make amends.
I'll hate my wife yet more, damn her! I'll part with her, rob 220
her of all she's worth, and we'll retire somewhere, anywhere,

221. we'll retire] *W1;* will retire *Q1.*

to another world. I'll marry thee; be pacified. 'Sdeath, they
come; hide your face, your tears. You have a mask; wear it
a moment. This way, this way. Be persuaded.   *Exeunt.*

Enter Mirabell *and* Mrs. Fainall.

MRS. FAINALL.

They are here yet.   225

MIRABELL.

They are turning into the other walk.

MRS. FAINALL.

While I only hated my husband, I could bear to see him;
but since I have despised him, he's too offensive.

MIRABELL.

Oh, you should hate with prudence.

MRS. FAINALL.

Yes, for I have loved with indiscretion.   230

MIRABELL.

You should have just so much disgust for your husband as
may be sufficient to make you relish your lover.

MRS. FAINALL.

You have been the cause that I have loved without bounds,
and would you set limits to that aversion of which you have
been the occasion? Why did you make me marry this man? 235

MIRABELL.

Why do we daily commit disagreeable and dangerous
actions? To save that idol, reputation. If the familiarities
of our loves had produced that consequence of which you
were apprehensive, where could you have fixed a father's
name with credit, but on a husband? I knew Fainall to be a 240
man lavish of his morals, an interested and professing friend,
a false and a designing lover; yet one whose wit and outward
fair behavior have gained a reputation with the town enough
to make that woman stand excused who has suffered herself
to be won by his addresses. A better man ought not to have 245
been sacrificed to the occasion; a worse had not answered to

---

222. *'Sdeath*] a contraction of *God's death*.
223. *mask*] a covering of silk or velvet, with openings for the eyes, con-
cealing the upper part of the face and worn for disguise.
241. *interested and professing*] self-interested and making a pretense (of
friendship).

the purpose. When you are weary of him, you know your
remedy.

MRS. FAINALL.

I ought to stand in some degree of credit with you,
Mirabell.   250

MIRABELL.

In justice to you, I have made you privy to my whole design,
and put it in your power to ruin or advance my fortune.

MRS. FAINALL.

Whom have you instructed to represent your pretended
uncle?

MIRABELL.

Waitwell, my servant.   255

MRS. FAINALL.

He is an humble servant to Foible, my mother's woman,
and may win her to your interest.

MIRABELL.

Care is taken for that. She is won and worn by this time.
They were married this morning.

MRS. FAINALL.

Who?   260

MIRABELL.

Waitwell and Foible. I would not tempt my servant to
betray me by trusting him too far. If your mother, in
hopes to ruin me, should consent to marry my pretended
uncle, he might, like Mosca in *The Fox*, stand upon terms;
so I made him sure beforehand.   265

MRS. FAINALL.

So, if my poor mother is caught in a contract, you will
discover the imposture betimes, and release her by producing
a certificate of her gallant's former marriage.

MIRABELL.

Yes, upon condition she consent to my marriage with her
niece, and surrender the moiety of her fortune in her   270
possession.

269. *upon condition she*] *Q1; upon
condition that she W1.*

---

251. *privy to*] privately aware of.
264. *like Mosca . . . terms*] In Jonson's *Volpone* (1606) the clever parasite,
Mosca, threatens to expose his master if the latter will not give him half
of his wealth.

MRS. FAINALL.

She talked last night of endeavoring at a match between
Millamant and your uncle.

MIRABELL.

That was by Foible's direction, and my instruction, that
she might seem to carry it more privately.   275

MRS. FAINALL.

Well, I have an opinion of your success, for I believe my
lady will do anything to get a husband; and when she has
this, which you have provided for her, I suppose she will
submit to anything to get rid of him.

MIRABELL.

Yes, I think the good lady would marry anything that 280
resembled a man, though 'twere no more than what a butler
could pinch out of a napkin.

MRS. FAINALL.

Female frailty! We must all come to it, if we live to be old
and feel the craving of a false appetite when the true is
decayed.   285

MIRABELL.

An old woman's appetite is depraved like that of a girl.
'Tis the green sickness of a second childhood; and like the
faint offer of a latter spring, serves but to usher in the fall,
and withers in an affected bloom.

MRS. FAINALL.

Here's your mistress.   290

Enter Mrs. Millamant, Witwoud, *and* Mincing.

MIRABELL.

Here she comes, i'faith, full sail, with her fan spread and
her streamers out, and a shoal of fools for tenders. Ha,

291–292. and her streamers] *Q1;* and
streamers *W1.*

---

275. *carry it*] carry on the business.

281–282. *what a butler could pinch out of a napkin*] i.e., in a fancy shape
for a dinner table.

287. *green sickness*] an anemic disease of young women.

291. *i'faith, full sail*] In Dryden's *An Evening's Love* (1663) Wildblood
says of Jacintha, as she approaches: "Yonder she comes, with full sails
i'faith!"

292. *streamers*] flags, i.e., the lappets of her headdress.

no, I cry her mercy!

MRS. FAINALL.

I see but one poor empty sculler; and he tows her woman
after him.   295

MIRABELL.

You seem to be unattended, madam. You used to have the
beau monde throng after you, and a flock of gay fine perukes
hovering round you.

WITWOUD.

Like moths about a candle. I had like to have lost my
comparison for want of breath.   300

MILLAMANT.

Oh, I have denied myself airs today. I have walked as fast
through the crowd—

WITWOUD.

As a favorite in disgrace, and with as few followers.

MILLAMANT.

Dear Mr. Witwoud, truce with your similitudes; for I am
as sick of 'em—   305

WITWOUD.

As a physician of a good air. I cannot help it, madam,
though 'tis against myself.

MILLAMANT.

Yet again! Mincing, stand between me and his wit.

WITWOUD.

Do, Mrs. Mincing, like a screen before a great fire. I
confess I do blaze today; I am too bright.   310

MRS. FAINALL.

But, dear Millamant, why were you so long?

MILLAMANT.

Long! Lord, have I not made violent haste? I have asked
every living thing I met for you; I have inquired after
you, as after a new fashion.

WITWOUD.

Madam, truce with your similitudes. No, you met her 315

---

303. in disgrace] *Q1;* just dis-
graced *W1.*

---

294. *sculler*] a single rower of a boat with two sculls, or short oars.
297. *perukes*] wigs.   304. *similitudes*] comparisons.

husband, and did not ask him for her.

MIRABELL.

By your leave, Witwoud, that were like inquiring after an old fashion, to ask a husband for his wife.

WITWOUD.

Hum, a hit! a hit! a palpable hit! I confess it.

MRS. FAINALL.

You were dressed before I came abroad.   320

MILLAMANT.

Aye, that's true. Oh, but then I had—Mincing, what had I? Why was I so long?

MINCING.

O mem, your la'ship stayed to peruse a pecquet of letters.

MILLAMANT.

Oh, aye, letters; I had letters. I am persecuted with letters. I hate letters. Nobody knows how to write letters; and yet 325 one has 'em, one does not know why. They serve one to pin up one's hair.

WITWOUD.

Is that the way? Pray, madam, do you pin up your hair with all your letters? I find I must keep copies.

MILLAMANT.

Only with those in verse, Mr. Witwoud. I never pin up my 330 hair with prose. I fancy one's hair would not curl if it were pinned up with prose. I think I tried once, Mincing.

MINCING.

O mem, I shall never forget it.

MILLAMANT.

Aye, poor Mincing tift and tift all the morning.

MINCING.

'Till I had the cremp in my fingers, I'll vow, mem. And 335 all to no purpose. But when your la'ship pins it up with poetry, it sits so pleasant the next day as anything, and is so pure and so crips.

---

323. pecquet] *Q1;* pacquet *Q2, W1.*   *omitted in Q2, W1.*
331–332. I fancy . . . prose] *Q1;*   335. cremp] *Q1;* cramp *Q2, W1.*

---

319. *a palpable hit*] an easily perceptible, effectively turned phrase.
323. *mem*] contraction of *madam.*   323. *la'ship*] i.e., ladyship.
323. *pecquet*] packet.   334. *tift*] patted and arranged (her hair).
335. *cremp*] cramp.   338. *crips*] a variation of crisp.

WITWOUD.

Indeed, so crips?

MINCING.

You're such a critic, Mr. Witwoud.   340

MILLAMANT.

Mirabell, did not you take exceptions last night? Oh, aye,
and went away. Now I think on't, I'm angry. No, now I
think on't, I'm pleased; for I believe I gave you some pain.

MIRABELL.

Does that please you?

MILLAMANT.

Infinitely; I love to give pain.   345

MIRABELL.

You would affect a cruelty which is not in your nature;
your true vanity is in the power of pleasing.

MILLAMANT.

Oh, I ask your pardon for that. One's cruelty is one's power;
and when one parts with one's cruelty, one parts with
one's power; and when one has parted with that, I fancy 350
one's old and ugly.

MIRABELL.

Aye, aye, suffer your cruelty to ruin the object of your
power, to destroy your lover, and then how vain, how lost
a thing you'll be! Nay, 'tis true: you are no longer handsome
when you've lost your lover; your beauty dies upon the 355
instant. For beauty is the lover's gift; 'tis he bestows your
charms, your glass is all a cheat. The ugly and the old, whom
the looking glass mortifies, yet after commendation can be
flattered by it, and discover beauties in it; for that reflects
our praises, rather than your face.   360

MILLAMANT.

Oh, the vanity of these men! Fainall, d'ye hear him? If
they did not commend us, we were not handsome! Now you
must know they could not commend one, if one was not
handsome. Beauty the lover's gift! Lord, what is a lover,
that it can give? Why, one makes lovers as fast as one pleases, 365
and they live as long as one pleases, and they die as soon as
one pleases; and then, if one pleases, one makes more.

341. did not] *Q1;* not *omitted in W1.*

WITWOUD.

> Very pretty. Why, you make no more of making of lovers,
> madam, than of making so many card-matches.

MILLAMANT.

> One no more owes one's beauty to a lover than one's wit to 370
> an echo. They can but reflect what we look and say; vain
> empty things if we are silent or unseen, and want a being.

MIRABELL.

> Yet to those two vain empty things you owe two [of] the
> greatest pleasures of your life.

MILLAMANT.

> How so?   375

MIRABELL.

> To your lover you owe the pleasure of hearing yourselves
> praised; and to an echo the pleasure of hearing yourselves
> talk.

WITWOUD.

> But I know a lady that loves talking so incessantly, she won't
> give an echo fair play; she has that everlasting rotation of 380
> tongue, that an echo must wait till she dies, before it can
> catch her last words.

MILLAMANT.

> Oh, fiction! Fainall, let us leave these men.

MIRABELL.

> Draw off Witwoud.   (*Aside to* Mrs. Fainall.)

MRS. FAINALL.

> Immediately. I have a word or two for Mr. Witwoud.   385
> > *Exeunt* Witwoud *and* Mrs. Fainall.

MIRABELL.

> I would beg a little private audience too. You had the
> tyranny to deny me last night, though you knew I came to
> impart a secret to you that concerned my love.

MILLAMANT.

> You saw I was engaged.

MIRABELL.

> Unkind! You had the leisure to entertain a herd of fools; 390
> things who visit you from their excessive idleness, bestowing

---

369. *card-matches*] pieces of cardboard dipped in melted sulphur and
used as matches.

on your easiness that time which is the incumbrance of
their lives. How can you find delight in such society? It is
impossible they should admire you; they are not capable.
Or if they were, it should be to you as a mortification, for 395
sure to please a fool is some degree of folly.

MILLAMANT.

I please myself. Besides, sometimes to converse with fools
is for my health.

MIRABELL.

Your health! Is there a worse disease than the conversation
of fools?   400

MILLAMANT.

Yes, the vapors; fools are physic for it, next to assafoetida.

MIRABELL.

You are not in a course of fools?

MILLAMANT.

Mirabell, if you persist in this offensive freedom, you'll
displease me. I think I must resolve, after all, not to have
you; we shan't agree.   405

MIRABELL.

Not in our physic, it may be.

MILLAMANT.

And yet our distemper, in all likelihood, will be the same;
for we shall be sick of one another. I shan't endure to be
reprimanded nor instructed; 'tis so dull to act always by
advice, and so tedious to be told of one's faults—I can't bear 410
it. Well, I won't have you, Mirabell—I'm resolved—I think
—you may go. —Ha! ha! ha! What would you give that you
could help loving me?

MIRABELL.

I would give something that you did not know I could not
help it.   415

MILLAMANT.

Come, don't look grave then. Well, what do you say to me?

MIRABELL.

I say that a man may as soon make a friend by his wit, or a

---

392. *easiness*] indulgence.
401. *assafoetida*] a gum resin used in medicine to prevent spasms.
402. *a course of fools*] a cure of fools, in place of medicine, for low spirits.

fortune by his honesty, as win a woman with plain dealing
and sincerity.

MILLAMANT.

Sententious Mirabell! Prithee, don't look with that violent 420
and inflexible wise face, like Solomon at the dividing of the
child in an old tapestry hanging.

MIRABELL.

You are merry, madam, but I would persuade you for one
moment to be serious.

MILLAMANT.

What, with that face? No, if you keep your countenance, 425
'tis impossible I should hold mine. Well, after all, there is
something very moving in a love-sick face. Ha! ha! ha!
—Well, I won't laugh, don't be peevish—Heighho! Now I'll
be melancholy, as melancholy as a watch-light. Well, Mirabell, if ever you will win me, woo me now. —Nay, if you are 430
so tedious, fare you well. —I see they are walking away.

MIRABELL.

Can you not find in the variety of your disposition one
moment—

MILLAMANT.

To hear you tell me Foible's married, and your plot like
to speed? —No.   435

MIRABELL.

But how came you to know it?

MILLAMANT.

Unless by the help of the devil, you can't imagine; unless
she should tell me herself. Which of the two it may have
been, I will leave you to consider; and when you have done
thinking of that, think of me.   *Exit* [*with* Mincing]. 440

MIRABELL.

I have something more—Gone! Think of you! To think of
a whirlwind, though 'twere in a whirlwind, were a case of
more steady contemplation; a very tranquility of mind and
mansion. A fellow that lives in a windmill has not a more

430. woo] *Q2, W1;* woe *Q1.*   437. Unless by the help] *Q1;* with-
                                        out the help *W1.*

421–422. *like Solomon . . . child*] cf. I Kings 3:16–28.
429. *watch-light*] night-light, or slow-burning candle.

whimsical dwelling than the heart of a man that is lodged 445
in a woman. There is no point of the compass to which
they cannot turn, and by which they are not turned; and
by one as well as another, for motion, not method, is their
occupation. To know this, and yet continue to be in love, is
to be made wise from the dictates of reason, and yet per- 450
severe to play the fool by the force of instinct. —Oh, here
come my pair of turtles! —What, billing so sweetly! Is not
Valentine's Day over with you yet?

Enter Waitwell *and* Foible.

Sirrah, Waitwell, why sure you think you were married for
your own recreation, and not for my conveniency.   455

WAITWELL.

Your pardon, sir. With submission, we have indeed been
solacing in lawful delights; but still with an eye to business,
sir. I have instructed her as well as I could. If she can
take your directions as readily as my instructions, sir, your
affairs are in a prosperous way.   460

MIRABELL.

Give you joy, Mrs. Foible.

FOIBLE.

O las, sir, I'm so ashamed! I'm afraid my lady has been in a
thousand inquietudes for me. But I protest, sir, I made as
much haste as I could.

WAITWELL.

That she did indeed, sir. It was my fault that she did not 465
make more.

MIRABELL.

That I believe.

FOIBLE.

But I told my lady as you instructed me, sir, that I had a
prospect of seeing Sir Rowland, your uncle; and that I would
put her ladyship's picture in my pocket to show him, which 470
I'll be sure to say has made him so enamored of her beauty,
that he burns with impatience to lie at her ladyship's feet and
worship the original.

---

452. *turtles*] turtle doves.
462. *O las*] Alas.

MIRABELL.

Excellent Foible! Matrimony has made you eloquent in
love.   475

WAITWELL.

I think she has profited, sir. I think so.

FOIBLE.

You have seen Madam Millamant, sir?

MIRABELL.

Yes.

FOIBLE.

I told her, sir, because I did not know that you might find
an opportunity; she had so much company last night.   480

MIRABELL.

Your diligence will merit more. In the meantime—

Gives money.

FOIBLE.

O dear sir, your humble servant.

WAITWELL.

Spouse.

MIRABELL.

Stand off, sir, not a penny! Go on and prosper, Foible; the
lease shall be made good and the farm stocked, if we   485
succeed.

FOIBLE.

I don't question your generosity, sir; and you need not
doubt of success. If you have no more commands, sir,
I'll be gone; I'm sure my lady is at her toilet and can't dress
till I come. —Oh dear, I'm sure that *(looking out)* was 490
Mrs. Marwood that went by in a mask; if she has seen me
with you I'm sure she'll tell my lady. I'll make haste
home and prevent her. Your servant, sir. B'w'y, Waitwell.

Exit.

WAITWELL.

Sir Rowland, if you please. The jade's so pert upon her
preferment she forgets herself.   495

---

483. *Spouse*] Waitwell attempts to take from Foible the money which
Mirabell has given her.

493. *B'w'y*] contraction of *God be with you* or *Good-by.*

494. *jade*] hussy.

MIRABELL.

Come, sir, will you endeavor to forget yourself, and transform into Sir Rowland?

WAITWELL.

Why, sir, it will be impossible I should remember myself. Married, knighted, and attended all in one day! 'Tis enough to make any man forget himself. The difficulty will be how to 500 recover my acquaintance and familiarity with my former self, and fall from my transformation to a reformation into Waitwell. Nay, I shan't be quite the same Waitwell neither; for now I remember me, I am married and can't be my own man again.   505

    Aye, there's the grief; that's the sad change of life,
    To lose my title, and yet keep my wife.   *Exeunt.*

[III]   *A Room in* Lady Wishfort's *House.*
           Lady Wishfort *at her toilet*, Peg *waiting.*

LADY WISHFORT.

Merciful! no news of Foible yet?

PEG.

No, madam.

LADY WISHFORT.

I have no more patience. If I have not fretted myself till I am pale again, there's no veracity in me! Fetch me the red; the red, do you hear, sweetheart? An arrant ash-   5 color, as I'm a person! Look you how this wench stirs! Why dost thou not fetch me a little red? Didst thou not hear me, mopus?

PEG.

The red ratafia does your ladyship mean, or the cherry brandy?   10

LADY WISHFORT.

Ratafia, fool! No, fool! Not the ratafia, fool. Grant me patience! I mean the Spanish paper, idiot; complexion,

---

499. *attended*] waited for (with a pun upon *waited on*).
[III]
    1. *Merciful!*] Heaven (or God) understood.   5. *arrant*] complete.
    6. *a person*] a person of distinction.   8. *mopus*] stupid person.
    12. *Spanish paper*] a kind of rouge imported from Spain.

darling. Paint, paint, paint, dost thou understand that, changeling, dangling thy hands like bobbins before thee? Why dost thou not stir, puppet? thou wooden thing upon 15 wires!

PEG.

Lord, madam, your ladyship is so impatient! I cannot come at the paint, madam; Mrs. Foible has locked it up and carried the key with her.

LADY WISHFORT.

A pox take you both! Fetch me the cherry brandy then. 20 (*Exit* Peg.) I'm as pale and as faint, I look like Mrs. Qualmsick, the curate's wife, that's always breeding. Wench, come, come, wench, what art thou doing? sipping? tasting? Save thee, dost thou not know the bottle?

Re-enter Peg *with a bottle and china cup.*

PEG.

Madam, I was looking for a cup. 25

LADY WISHFORT.

A cup, save thee! and what a cup hast thou brought! Dost thou take me for a fairy, to drink out of an acorn? Why didst thou not bring thy thimble? Hast thou ne'er a brass thimble clinking in thy pocket with a bit of nutmeg? I warrant thee. Come, fill, fill! So; again. (*One knocks.*) 30 See who that is. Set down the bottle first. Here, here, under the table. What, wouldst thou go with the bottle in thy hand, like a tapster? As I'm a person, this wench has lived in an inn upon the road, before she came to me, like Maritornes the Asturian in *Don Quixote!* No Foible yet? 35

PEG.

No, madam, Mrs. Marwood.

LADY WISHFORT.

Oh, Marwood, let her come in. Come in, good Marwood.

---

14. *changeling*] child secretly exchanged in infancy for a more desirable one, hence an idiot.

14. *bobbins*] small wooden pins with a notch, to wind thread about in weaving or sewing.

29. *brass thimble . . . nutmeg*] as good luck charms.

35. *Maritornes the Asturian*] an ill-favored chambermaid who brings a jug of water to revive Sancho in Cervantes' *Don Quixote.*

Enter Mrs. Marwood.

MRS. MARWOOD.

I'm surprised to find your ladyship in dishabillé at this
time of day.

LADY WISHFORT.

Foible's a lost thing; has been abroad since morning, and   40
never heard of since.

MRS. MARWOOD.

I saw her but now, as I came masked through the park, in
conference with Mirabell.

LADY WISHFORT.

With Mirabell! You call my blood into my face with
mentioning that traitor. She durst not have the confidence!   45
I sent her to negotiate an affair in which, if I'm detected, I'm
undone. If that wheedling villain has wrought upon Foible
to detect me, I'm ruined. Oh my dear friend, I'm a wretch
of wretches if I'm detected.

MRS. MARWOOD.

O madam, you cannot suspect Mrs. Foible's integrity.   50

LADY WISHFORT.

Oh, he carries poison in his tongue that would corrupt
integrity itself! If she has given him an opportunity, she has
as good as put her integrity into his hands. Ah, dear
Marwood, what's integrity to an opportunity? Hark! I hear
her! Go, you thing, and send her in.   (*Exit* Peg.)   Dear   55
friend, retire into my closet, that I may examine her with
more freedom. You'll pardon me, dear friend; I can make
bold with you. There are books over the chimney. Quarles
and Prynne, and the *Short View of the Stage*, with Bunyan's
works, to entertain you.   *Exit* Mrs. Marwood.   60

38. dishabillé] *Q2, W1;* dishabi-   55. *W1 places* Go . . . in! *at the end*
lie *Q1.*   *of this speech.*

---

56. *closet*] small room for privacy.

58. *Quarles*] Francis Quarles, a religious poet, author of *Emblems, Divine
and Moral* (1635).

59. *Prynne*] William Prynne, author of *Histrio-Mastix* (1633), a Puritan
attack on the stage.

59. *Short View of the Stage*] In *A Short View of the Immorality and Profaneness
of the English Stage* (1698) the author, Jeremy Collier, an Anglican clergy-
man, had included an attack on Congreve's earlier plays.

59–60. *Bunyan's works*] One volume of *The Works of that Eminent Servant
of Christ, Mr. John Bunyan*, had been published in 1692.

Enter Foible.

O Foible, where hast thou been? What hast thou been
doing?

FOIBLE.

Madam, I have seen the party.

LADY WISHFORT.

But what hast thou done?

FOIBLE.

Nay, 'tis your ladyship has done, and are to do; I have   65
only promised. But a man so enamored, so transported!
Well, here it is, all that is left; all that is not kissed away.
Well, if worshiping of pictures be a sin, poor Sir Rowland,
I say.

LADY WISHFORT.

The miniature has been counted like. But hast thou not   70
betrayed me, Foible? Hast thou not detected me to that
faithless Mirabell? What hadst thou to do with him in the
Park? Answer me, has he got nothing out of thee?

FOIBLE [*aside*].

So the devil has been beforehand with me. What shall I say?
—Alas, madam, could I help it, if I met that confident   75
thing? Was I in fault? If you had heard how he used me,
and all upon your ladyship's account, I'm sure you would
not suspect my fidelity. Nay, if that had been the worst, I
could have borne; but he had a fling at your ladyship too.
And then I could not hold; but i'faith I gave him his own.   80

LADY WISHFORT.

Me? What did the filthy fellow say?

FOIBLE.

O madam! 'tis a shame to say what he said, with his taunts
and his fleers, tossing up his nose. Humph! (says he), what,
you are a hatching some plot (says he), you are so early
abroad, or catering (says he), ferreting for some disbanded   85
officer, I warrant. Half-pay is but thin subsistence (says he).
Well, what pension does your lady propose? Let me see

67. Well, here . . . away] *Q1;*
omitted in *Q2, W1.*

---

68. *if worshiping . . . sin*] the worship of religious pictures in Roman
Catholic churches.

83. *fleers*] sneers.

(says he), what, she must come down pretty deep now, she's
superannuated (says he) and—

LADY WISHFORT.

Ods my life, I'll have him, I'll have him murdered. I'll have   90
him poisoned. Where does he eat? I'll marry a drawer to
have him poisoned in his wine. I'll send for Robin from
Locket's immediately.

FOIBLE.

Poison him? Poisoning's too good for him. Starve him,
madam, starve him; marry Sir Rowland and get him   95
disinherited. Oh, you would bless yourself to hear what he
said!

LADY WISHFORT.

A villain! superannuated!

FOIBLE.

Humph! (says he), I hear you are laying designs against
me too (says he), and Mrs. Millamant is to marry my uncle   100
(he does not suspect a word of your ladyship); but (says he)
I'll fit you for that. I warrant you (says he), I'll hamper you
for that (says he), you and your old frippery too (says he),
I'll handle you—

LADY WISHFORT.

Audacious villain! Handle me! would he durst! Frippery?   105
old frippery! Was there ever such a foulmouthed fellow?
I'll be married tomorrow; I'll be contracted tonight.

FOIBLE.

The sooner the better, madam.

LADY WISHFORT.

Will Sir Rowland be here, say'st thou? When, Foible?

FOIBLE.

Incontinently, madam. No new sheriff's wife expects the   110
return of her husband after knighthood with that impatience
in which Sir Rowland burns for the dear hour of kissing
your ladyship's hands after dinner.

113. hands] *Q1;* hand *Q2, W1.*

---

90. *Ods*] a contraction of *God's.*   91. *drawer*] waiter.
93. *Locket's*] a fashionable tavern in Charing Cross.
103. *frippery*] cast-off garments.
110. *incontinently*] immediately.

LADY WISHFORT.

Frippery? superannuated frippery! I'll frippery the villain;
I'll reduce him to frippery and rags! A tatterdemalion! I 115
hope to see him hung with tatters, like a Long Lane penthouse or a gibbet thief. A slander-mouthed railer! I
warrant the spendthrift prodigal's in debt as much as the
million lottery, or the whole court upon a birthday. I'll
spoil his credit with his tailor. Yes, he shall have my niece 120
with her fortune, he shall!

FOIBLE.

He! I hope to see him lodge in Ludgate first, and angle
into Blackfriars for brass farthings with an old mitten.

LADY WISHFORT.

Aye, dear Foible; thank thee for that, dear Foible. He has
put me out of all patience. I shall never recompose my 125
features to receive Sir Rowland with any economy of face.
This wretch has fretted me that I am absolutely decayed.
Look, Foible.

FOIBLE.

Your ladyship has frowned a little too rashly, indeed,
madam. There are some cracks discernible in the white 130
varnish.

LADY WISHFORT.

Let me see the glass. Cracks, say'st thou? Why I am
arrantly flayed; I look like an old peeled wall. Thou must
repair me, Foible, before Sir Rowland comes, or I shall

133. flayed] *Spelled* flea'd *Q1-2, W1.*

---

115. *tatterdemalion*] ragged fellow.

116–117. *Long Lane penthouse*] stall under an overhanging roof in Long
Lane, where rags were sold.

118–119. *the million lottery*] a government scheme to raise a million pounds
by the sale of lottery tickets.

119. *court . . . birthday*] Courtiers were expected to wear new and expensive
clothes on the sovereign's birthday.

122. *Ludgate*] Ludgate Prison in Blackfriars, chiefly used for debtors.

122–123. *angle . . . mitten*] Debtors in Ludgate Prison were in the
habit of begging alms of passers-by through a grating. By means of a mitten
let down on a string from an upper window contributions could be drawn
up.

126. *economy*] orderly arrangement.

never keep up to my picture.

FOIBLE.

I warrant you, madam, a little art once made your picture
like you; and now a little of the same art must make you
like your picture. Your picture must sit for you, madam.

LADY WISHFORT.

But art thou sure Sir Rowland will not fail to come? Or
will he not fail when he does come? Will he be importunate, 140
Foible, and push? For if he should not be importunate, I
shall never break decorums. I shall die with confusion, if I
am forced to advance. Oh no, I can never advance! I shall
swoon if he should expect advances. No, I hope Sir Rowland is better bred than to put a lady to the necessity of 145
breaking her forms. I won't be too coy neither. I won't give
him despair; but a little disdain is not amiss, a little scorn is
alluring.

FOIBLE.

A little scorn becomes your ladyship.

LADY WISHFORT.

Yes, but tenderness becomes me best, a sort of a dyingness. 150
You see that picture has a sort of a—ha, Foible? a swim-
mingness in the eyes. Yes, I'll look so. My niece affects it;
but she wants features. Is Sir Rowland handsome? Let my
toilet be removed. I'll dress above. I'll receive Sir Rowland
here. Is he handsome? Don't answer me. I won't know; I'll 155
be surprised, I'll be taken by surprise.

FOIBLE.

By storm, madam. Sir Rowland's a brisk man.

LADY WISHFORT.

Is he! Oh, then he'll importune, if he's a brisk man.
I shall save decorums if Sir Rowland importunes. I have
a mortal terror at the apprehension of offending against 160
decorums. Nothing but importunity can surmount decorums.
Oh, I'm glad he's a brisk man. Let my things be removed,
good Foible.   *Exit.*

151–152. swimmingness] *Q2, W1;*   161. Nothing . . . decorums] *Q1;*
swimminess *Q1.*   omitted in *Q2, W1.*

---

142. *break decorums*] violate propriety.
153. *wants*] lacks.

Enter Mrs. Fainall.

MRS. FAINALL.

O Foible, I have been in a fright, lest I should come too
late! That devil Marwood saw you in the Park with Mira- 165
bell, and I'm afraid will discover it to my lady.

FOIBLE.

Discover what, madam?

MRS. FAINALL.

Nay, nay, put not on that strange face. I am privy to the
whole design, and know that Waitwell, to whom thou wert
this morning married, is to personate Mirabell's uncle, and 170
as such, winning my lady, to involve her in those difficulties
from which Mirabell only must release her, by his making
his conditions to have my cousin and her fortune left to her
own disposal.

FOIBLE.

O dear madam, I beg your pardon. It was not my confidence 175
in your ladyship that was deficient; but I thought the former
good correspondence between your ladyship and Mr. Mirabell might have hindered his communicating this secret.

MRS. FAINALL.

Dear Foible, forget that.

FOIBLE.

O dear madam, Mr. Mirabell is such a sweet, winning 180
gentleman, but your ladyship is the pattern of generosity.
Sweet lady, to be so good! Mr. Mirabell cannot choose but
be grateful. I find your ladyship has his heart still. Now,
madam, I can safely tell your ladyship our success. Mrs.
Marwood had told my lady; but I warrant I managed myself. 185
I turned it all for the better. I told my lady that Mr. Mirabell railed at her. I laid horrid things to his charge, I'll vow;
and my lady is so incensed that she'll be contracted to Sir
Rowland tonight, she says. I warrant I worked her up, that
he may have her for asking for, as they say of a Welsh 190
maidenhead.

MRS. FAINALL.

O rare Foible!

---

170. *personate*] impersonate.

FOIBLE.

Madam, I beg your ladyship to acquaint Mr. Mirabell of
his success. I would be seen as little as possible to speak to
him; besides, I believe Madame Marwood watches me. 195
She has a month's mind; but I know Mr. Mirabell can't
abide her. (*Enter* Footman.) John, remove my lady's
toilet. Madam, your servant. My lady is so impatient,
I fear she'll come for me, if I stay.

MRS. FAINALL.

I'll go with you up the backstairs, lest I should meet her.   200
Exeunt.

Enter Mrs. Marwood.

MRS. MARWOOD.

Indeed, Mrs. Engine, is it thus with you? Are you become a
go-between of this importance? Yes, I shall watch you. Why
this wench is the *passe-partout*, a very master key to everybody's strongbox. My friend Fainall, have you carried it so
swimmingly? I thought there was something in it; but it 205
seems it's over with you. Your loathing is not from a want of
appetite then, but from a surfeit. Else you could never be so
cool to fall from a principal to be an assistant; to procure
for him! A pattern of generosity, that I confess. Well, Mr.
Fainall, you have met with your match. O man, man! 210
woman, woman! The devil's an ass; if I were a painter, I
would draw him like an idiot, a driveler with a bib and
bells. Man should have his head and horns, and woman the
rest of him. Poor simple fiend! Madam Marwood has a
month's mind, but he can't abide her. 'Twere better for him 215
you had not been his confessor in that affair, without you
could have kept his counsel closer. I shall not prove
another pattern of generosity and stalk for him, till he takes
his stand to aim at a fortune. He has not obliged me to that,

218–219. and stalk . . . fortune] *Q1;*
omitted in *W1.*

196. *month's mind*] strong inclination.
201. *Mrs. Engine*] Mrs. Trickery.
203. *passe-partout*] key that opens any door.
212. *driveler*] one who talks in a foolish way.
213. *horns*] referring to the horns which were imagined to sprout on
the head of a cuckold.

with those excesses of himself; and now I'll have none of 220
him. Here comes the good lady, panting ripe; with a heart
full of hope, and a head full of care, like any chemist upon
the day of projection.

Enter Lady Wishfort.

LADY WISHFORT.

O dear Marwood, what shall I say, for this rude forget-
fulness? But my dear friend is all goodness.   225

MRS. MARWOOD.

No apologies, dear madam. I have been very well entertained.

LADY WISHFORT.

As I'm a person, I am in a very chaos to think I should so
forget myself; but I have such an olio of affairs, really I know
not what to do. —(*Calls.*)   Foible! —I expect my nephew, 230
Sir Wilfull, every moment too. —Why, Foible! —He
means to travel for improvement.

MRS. MARWOOD.

Methinks Sir Wilfull should rather think of marrying than
traveling at his years. I hear he is turned of forty.

LADY WISHFORT.

Oh, he's in less danger of being spoiled by his travels. I 235
am against my nephew's marrying too young. It will be
time enough when he comes back and has acquired discretion to choose for himself.

MRS. MARWOOD.

Methinks Mrs. Millamant and he would make a very
fit match. He may travel afterwards. 'Tis a thing very 240
usual with young gentlemen.

LADY WISHFORT.

I promise you I have thought on't; and since 'tis your
judgment, I'll think on't again. I assure you I will; I value
your judgment extremely. On my word, I'll propose it.

---

223. *projection*] the final process of alchemy in the attempt to transmute
base metal into gold.
228. *chaos*] utter disorder.
229. *olio*] hodgepodge.

Enter Foible.

Come, come, Foible, I had forgot my nephew will be here 245
before dinner. I must make haste.

FOIBLE.

Mr. Witwoud and Mr. Petulant are come to dine with your
ladyship.

LADY WISHFORT.

Oh dear, I can't appear till I'm dressed. Dear Marwood,
shall I be free with you again, and beg you to entertain 'em? 250
I'll make all imaginable haste. Dear friend, excuse me.

Exeunt Lady Wishfort *and* Foible.

Enter Mrs. Millamant *and* Mincing.

MILLAMANT.

Sure never anything was so unbred as that odious man!
Marwood, your servant.

MRS. MARWOOD.

You have a color, what's the matter?

MILLAMANT.

That horrid fellow, Petulant, has provoked me into a flame. 255
I have broke my fan. Mincing, lend me yours; is not all
the powder out of my hair?

MRS. MARWOOD.

No, what has he done?

MILLAMANT.

Nay, he has done nothing; he has only talked. Nay, he has
said nothing neither; but he has contradicted everything 260
that has been said. For my part, I thought Witwoud and he
would have quarreled.

MINCING.

I vow, mem, I thought once they would have fit.

MILLAMANT.

Well, 'tis a lamentable thing, I'll swear, that one has not the
liberty of choosing one's acquaintance as one does one's 265
clothes.

264. I'll swear] *Q1;* I swear *Q2,*
W1.

263. *fit*] fought.

MRS. MARWOOD.

If we had the liberty, we should be as weary of one set of
acquaintance, though never so good, as we are of one suit,
though never so fine. A fool and a doily stuff would now
and then find days of grace, and be worn for variety.   270

MILLAMANT.

I could consent to wear 'em, if they would wear alike; but
fools never wear out—they are such *drap-de-Berry* things
without one could give 'em to one's chambermaid after a day
or two!

MRS. MARWOOD.

'Twere better so indeed. Or what think you of the play- 275
house? A fine, gay, glossy fool should be given there, like a
new masking habit, after the masquerade is over, and we
have done with the disguise. For a fool's visit is always a
disguise, and never admitted by a woman of wit, but to blind
her affair with a lover of sense. If you would but appear 280
barefaced now, and own Mirabell, you might as easily put
off Petulant and Witwoud as your hood and scarf. And
indeed 'tis time, for the town has found it; the secret is
grown too big for the pretense. 'Tis like Mrs. Primly's great
belly; she may lace it down before, but it burnishes on her 285
hips. Indeed, Millamant, you can no more conceal it than
my Lady Strammel can her face, that goodly face, which,
in defiance of her Rhenish wine tea, will not be com-
prehended in a mask.

MILLAMANT.

I'll take my death, Marwood, you are more censorious 290
than a decayed beauty, or a discarded toast. Mincing, tell
the men they may come up. My aunt is not dressing [here].
—Their folly is less provoking than your malice. (*Exit*

292. dressing here] *W1;* here
omitted in Q1.

---

269. *doily stuff*] a light, cheap woollen cloth.
272. *drap-de-Berry*] coarse woollen cloth from the province of Berry
in France.
288. *Rhenish wine tea*] strong wine instead of tea. White Rhenish wine
was believed to reduce corpulence and correct a high color.
290. *I'll take my death*] I hope to die if what I say is untrue.
291. *discarded toast*] person whose health was formerly drunk.

Mincing.)   The town has found it! What has it found? That
Mirabell loves me is no more a secret than it is a secret that 295
you discovered it to my aunt, or than the reason why you
discovered it is a secret.

MRS. MARWOOD.
You are nettled.

MILLAMANT.
You're mistaken. Ridiculous!

MRS. MARWOOD.
Indeed, my dear, you'll tear another fan, if you don't 300
mitigate those violent airs.

MILLAMANT.
O silly! Ha! ha! ha! I could laugh immoderately. Poor
Mirabell! His constancy to me has quite destroyed his
complaisance for all the world beside. I swear, I never en-
joined it him to be so coy. If I had the vanity to think he 305
would obey me, I would command him to show more
gallantry. 'Tis hardly well-bred to be so particular on one
hand, and so insensible on the other. But I despair to
prevail, and so let him follow his own way. Ha! ha! ha!
Pardon me, dear creature, I must laugh, ha! ha! ha!— 310
though I grant you 'tis a little barbarous, ha! ha! ha!

MRS. MARWOOD.
What pity 'tis, so much fine raillery, and delivered with so
significant gesture, should be so unhappily directed to
miscarry.

MILLAMANT.
Ha? Dear creature, I ask your pardon. I swear I did not 315
mind you.

MRS. MARWOOD.
Mr. Mirabell and you both may think it a thing impossible,
when I shall tell him by telling you—

MILLAMANT.
Oh dear, what? For it is the same thing, if I hear it, ha!
ha! ha!   320

MRS. MARWOOD.
That I detest him, hate him, madam.

315. Ha] *Spelled* Hae *Q1–2, W1.*

316. *mind*] pay attention to.

MILLAMANT.

O madam, why so do I—and yet the creature loves me,
ha! ha! ha! How can one forbear laughing to think of it!
I am a sybil if I am not amazed to think what he can see in
me. I'll take my death, I think you are handsomer—and 325
within a year or two as young. If you could but stay for
me, I should overtake you—but that cannot be. —Well,
that thought makes me melancholy. —Now I'll be sad.

MRS. MARWOOD.

Your merry note may be changed sooner than you think.

MILLAMANT.

D'ye say so? Then I'm resolved to have a song to keep up 330
my spirits.

Enter Mincing.

MINCING.

The gentlemen stay but to comb, madam, and will wait
on you.

MILLAMANT.

Desire Mrs. ——, that is in the next room, to sing the
song I would have learned yesterday. You shall hear it, 335
madam, not that there's any great matter in it, but 'tis agreeable to my humor.

Song
Set by Mr. John Eccles *and sung by* Mrs. Hodgson.

I

Love's but the frailty of the mind,
When 'tis not with ambition joined;
A sickly flame, which, if not fed, expires,
And feeding, wastes in self-consuming fires. 340

II

'Tis not to wound a wanton boy
Or amorous youth, that gives the joy;
But 'tis the glory to have pierced a swain,
For whom inferior beauties sighed in vain. 345

---

328. melancholy] *Q1–2;* melan-   337.2 and ... Hodgson] *Q1; omitted*
cholick *W1.*   *in W1.*

---

324. *sybil*] prophetess.
332. *comb*] i.e., their wigs.

III

Then I alone the conquest prize,
When I insult a rival's eyes;
If there's delight in love, 'tis when I see
That heart, which others bleed for, bleed for me.

Enter Petulant *and* Witwoud.

MILLAMANT.

Is your animosity composed, gentlemen?   350

WITWOUD.

Raillery, raillery, madam; we have no animosity. We hit off
a little wit now and then, but no animosity. The falling-out
of wits is like the falling-out of lovers; we agree in the main,
like treble and bass. Ha, Petulant?

PETULANT.

Aye, in the main, but when I have a humor to contradict. 355

WITWOUD.

Aye, when he has a humor to contradict, then I contradict
too. What, I know my cue. Then we contradict one
another like two battledores; for contradictions beget one
another like Jews.

PETULANT.

If he says black's black, if I have a humor to say 'tis blue, 360
let that pass; all's one for that. If I have a humor to
prove it, it must be granted.

WITWOUD.

Not positively must, but it may, it may.

PETULANT.

Yes, it positively must, upon proof positive.

WITWOUD.

Aye, upon proof positive it must; but upon proof pre- 365
sumptive it only may. That's a logical distinction now,
madam.

MRS. MARWOOD.

I perceive your debates are of importance and very
learnedly handled.

_____

353. *in the main*] the mean, the middle or tenor part, with which the other
two harmonize; also in the sense of *mainly*.
358. *battledores*] two who play with small rackets, as they strike a shuttle-
cock to and from each other.

PETULANT.

Importance is one thing, and learning's another; but a 370
debate's a debate, that I assert.

WITWOUD.

Petulant's an enemy to learning; he relies altogether on
his parts.

PETULANT.

No, I'm no enemy to learning; it hurts not me.

MRS. MARWOOD.

That's a sign indeed it's no enemy to you. 375

PETULANT.

No, no, it's no enemy to anybody but them that have it.

MILLAMANT.

Well, an illiterate man's my aversion. I wonder at the impudence of any illiterate man to offer to make love.

WITWOUD.

That I confess I wonder at too.

MILLAMANT.

Ah! to marry an ignorant that can hardly read or write! 380

PETULANT.

Why should a man be ever the further from being married,
though he can't read, any more than he is from being
hanged? The ordinary's paid for setting the psalm, and
the parish priest for reading the ceremony. And for the
rest which is to follow in both cases, a man may do it 385
without book; so all's one for that.

MILLAMANT.

D'ye hear the creature? Lord, here's company, I'll be gone.

Exeunt Millamant *and* Mincing.

WITWOUD.

In the name of Bartlemew and his fair, what have we here?

MRS. MARWOOD.

'Tis your brother, I fancy. Don't you know him?

WITWOUD.

Not I. Yes, I think it is he. I've almost forgot him; I 390

382. any more] *Q1; omitted in W1.*

---

383. *The ordinary's paid . . . psalm*] A member of the clergy was appointed
to minister to condemned criminals.

388. *Bartlemew and his fair*] Bartholomew Fair was a popular fair held
annually in Smithfield on August 24, St. Bartholomew's Day.

have not seen him since the Revolution.

Enter Sir Wilfull Witwoud *in a country riding habit, and a* Servant *to* Lady Wishfort.

SERVANT.

Sir, my lady's dressing. Here's company; if you please to walk in, in the meantime.

SIR WILFULL.

Dressing! What, it's but morning here, I warrant, with you in London; we should count it towards afternoon in our 395 parts, down in Shropshire. Why then, belike my aunt han't dined yet, ha, friend?

SERVANT.

Your aunt, sir?

SIR WILFULL.

My aunt, sir! Yes, my aunt, sir, and your lady, sir; your lady is my aunt, sir. Why, what, dost thou not know me, 400 friend? Why then, send somebody here that does. How long hast thou lived with thy lady, fellow, ha?

SERVANT.

A week, sir; longer than anybody in the house, except my lady's woman.

SIR WILFULL.

Why then, belike thou dost not know thy lady, if thou seest 405 her, ha, friend?

SERVANT.

Why truly, sir, I cannot safely swear to her face in a morning, before she is dressed. 'Tis like I may give a shrewd guess at her by this time.

SIR WILFULL.

Well, prithee try what thou canst do; if thou canst not guess, 410 inquire her out, dost hear, fellow? And tell her, her nephew, Sir Wilfull Witwoud, is in the house.

SERVANT.

I shall, sir.

391.1 Servant] *Q1;* Footman *W1.*
So until Exit.

---

391. *the Revolution*] the Bloodless Revolution of 1688 which brought William and Mary to the throne.
405. *belike*] probably.

SIR WILFULL.

Hold ye, hear me, friend; a word **with** you in your ear.
Prithee who are these gallants?   415

SERVANT.

Really, sir, I can't tell; here come so many here, 'tis hard
to know 'em all.   *Exit* Servant.

SIR WILFULL.

Oons, this fellow knows less than a starling; I don't think a'
knows his own name.

MRS. MARWOOD.

Mr. Witwoud, your brother is not behindhand in forget- 420
fulness; I fancy he has forgot you too.

WITWOUD.

I hope so. The devil take him that remembers first, I say.

SIR WILFULL.

Save you, gentlemen and lady!

MRS. MARWOOD.

For shame, Mr. Witwoud; why won't you speak to him?
And you, sir.   425

WITWOUD.

Petulant, speak.

PETULANT.

And you, sir.

SIR WILFULL.

No offense, I hope.   *Salutes* Marwood.

MRS. MARWOOD.

No sure, sir.

WITWOUD.

This is a vile dog, I see that already. No offense! Ha! ha! 430
ha! to him; to him, Petulant, smoke him.

PETULANT.

It seems as if you had come a journey, sir; hem, hem.

                                        Surveying him round.

SIR WILFULL.

Very likely, sir, that it may seem so.

---

418. *Oons*] a corruption of *God's wounds*.
418. *starling*] considered a very stupid bird.
431. *smoke him*] make fun of him.

PETULANT.

No offense, I hope, sir.

WITWOUD.

Smoke the boots, the boots; Petulant, the boots, ha! ha! ha! 435

SIR WILFULL.

May be not, sir; thereafter as 'tis meant, sir.

PETULANT.

Sir, I presume upon the information of your boots.

SIR WILFULL.

Why, 'tis like you may, sir. If you are not satisfied with the
information of my boots, sir, if you will step to the stable,
you may inquire further of my horse, sir.   440

PETULANT.

Your horse, sir! Your horse is an ass, sir!

SIR WILFULL.

Do you speak by way of offense, sir?

MRS. MARWOOD.

The gentleman's merry, that's all, sir. —[Aside.] 'Slife,
we shall have a quarrel betwixt an horse and an ass, before
they find one another out. —[Aloud.] You must not take 445
anything amiss from your friends, sir. You are among your
friends here, though it may be you don't know it. If I am
not mistaken, you are Sir Wilfull Witwoud.

SIR WILFULL.

Right, lady; I am Sir Wilfull Witwoud, so I write myself;
no offense to anybody, I hope; and nephew to the Lady 450
Wishfort of this mansion.

MRS. MARWOOD.

Don't you know this gentleman, sir?

SIR WILFULL.

Hum! What, sure 'tis not—yea by'r Lady, but 'tis. 'Sheart,
I know not whether 'tis or no. Yea, but 'tis, by the Wrekin.
Brother Anthony! What, Tony, i'faith! What, dost thou 455
not know me? By'r Lady, nor I thee, thou art so be-cravated

455. Anthony] Q1; Antony W1.

---

436. thereafter] according.   443. 'Slife] a corruption of God's life.
453. 'Sheart] a corruption of God's heart.
454. Wrekin] a high hill near the center of Shropshire. "All friends
round the Wrekin" is a famous Shropshire toast.

and be-periwigged. 'Sheart, why dost not speak? Art thou
o'erjoyed?

WITWOUD.

Odso, brother, is it you? Your servant, brother.

SIR WILLFULL.

Your servant! Why, yours, sir. Your servant again, 'sheart, 460
and your friend and servant to that, and a—(*puff*) and a
flapdragon for your service, sir! and a hare's foot, and a
hare's scut for your service, sir, an you be so cold and so
courtly!

WITWOUD.

No offense, I hope, brother.   465

SIR WILFULL.

'Sheart, sir, but there is, and much offense! A pox, is this
your Inns o' Court breeding, not to know your friends and
your relations, your elders and your betters?

WITWOUD.

Why, brother Wilfull of Salop, you may be as short as a
Shrewsbury cake, if you please. But I tell you, 'tis not 470
modish to know relations in town. You think you're in the
country, where great lubberly brothers slabber and kiss one
another when they meet, like a call of serjeants. 'Tis not the
fashion here; 'tis not indeed, dear brother.

SIR WILFULL.

The fashion's a fool; and you're a fop, dear brother. 475
'Sheart, I've suspected this. By'r Lady, I conjectured you
were a fop, since you began to change the style of your letters
and write in a scrap of paper, gilt round the edges, no
broader than a subpoena. I might expect this when you

---

459. *Odso*] a variant of *Godso*, expressing surprise.

462. *flapdragon*] a raisin snatched from burning brandy and extinguished
by closing the mouth and swallowing, hence something valueless.

463. *hare's scut*] a term still in country use for a hare's tail.

467. *Inns o' Court*] the societies in London in which lawyers are trained
for the bar.

469. *Salop*] Shropshire.

470. *Shrewsbury cake*] a flat, round, biscuit-like cake. Shrewsbury is the
county town of Shropshire.

472. *slabber*] slobber.

473. *a call of serjeants*] a group of serjeants-at-law who had been raised
to that rank at the same time.

left off Honored Brother, and hoping you are in good health,   480
and so forth—to begin with a Rat me, knight, I'm so sick
of a last night's debauch—ods heart, and then tell a familiar
tale of a cock and a bull, and a whore and a bottle, and
so conclude. You could write news before you were
out of your time, when you lived with honest Pumple Nose,   485
the attorney of Furnival's Inn; you could entreat to be
remembered then to your friends round the Wrekin. We
could have gazettes then, and *Dawks's Letter*, and the
Weekly Bill, till of late days.

PETULANT.

'Slife, Witwoud, were you ever an attorney's clerk? of the   490
family of the Furnivals? Ha! ha! ha!

WITWOUD.

Aye, aye, but that was for a while, not long, not long.
Pshaw! I was not in my own power then; an orphan,
and this fellow was my guardian. Aye, aye, I was glad to
consent to that man to come to London. He had the   495
disposal of me then. If I had not agreed to that, I might have
been bound prentice to a felt-maker in Shrewsbury; this
fellow would have bound me to a maker of felts.

SIR WILFULL.

'Sheart, and better than to be bound to a maker of fops,
where, I suppose, you have served your time; and now you   500
may set up for yourself.

MRS. MARWOOD.

You intend to travel, sir, as I'm informed.

SIR WILFULL.

Belike I may, madam. I may chance to sail upon the salt

---

481. *Rat me*] an abbreviated form of *May God rot me*.
482. *ods heart*] a contraction of *God's heart*.
484–485. *before you were out of your time*] while you were still indentured
to an attorney.
485. *Pumple*] i.e., Pimple.
486. *Furnival's Inn*] a subordinate inn of court attached to Lincoln's Inn.
488. *gazettes*] news sheets.
488. *Dawks's Letter*] a weekly newsletter.
489. *Weekly Bill*] the official publication of deaths occurring in and
around London.
497. *bound prentice*] bound as an apprentice.

seas, if my mind hold.

PETULANT.

And the wind serve.   505

SIR WILFULL.

Serve or not serve, I shan't ask license of you, sir; nor the
weathercock your companion. I direct my discourse to the
lady, sir. 'Tis like my aunt may have told you, madam.
Yes, I have settled my concerns, I may say now, and am
minded to see foreign parts. If an how that the peace 510
holds, whereby, that is, taxes abate.

MRS. MARWOOD.

I thought you had designed for France at all adventures.

SIR WILFULL.

I can't tell that; 'tis like I may, and 'tis like I may not. I
am somewhat dainty in making a resolution, because when
I make it, I keep it. I don't stand shill I, shall I, then; if I 515
say't, I'll do't. But I have thoughts to tarry a small matter
in town, to learn somewhat of your lingo first, before I
cross the seas. I'd gladly have a spice of your French, as
they say, whereby to hold discourse in foreign countries.

MRS. MARWOOD.

Here is an academy in town for that use.   520

SIR WILFULL.

There is? 'Tis like there may.

MRS. MARWOOD.

No doubt you will return very much improved.

WITWOUD.

Yes, refined, like a Dutch skipper from a whale-fishing.

Enter Lady Wishfort *and* Fainall.

LADY WISHFORT.

Nephew, you are welcome.

SIR WILFULL.

Aunt, your servant.   525

510–511. *the peace holds*] The Peace of Ryswick (1697), which had
temporarily halted the war with France, was broken in 1701, the year
after this play was first acted.

512. *at all adventures*] at all costs.

515. *shill I, shall I*] shilly-shally, irresolute.

521. *'Tis like there may*] Very likely there is.

FAINALL.

Sir Wilfull, your most faithful servant.

SIR WILFULL.

Cousin Fainall, give me your hand.

LADY WISHFORT.

Cousin Witwoud, your servant; Mr. Petulant, your servant.
Nephew, you are welcome again. Will you drink anything
after your journey, nephew, before you eat? Dinner's 530
almost ready.

SIR WILFULL.

I'm very well, I thank you, aunt; however, I thank you
for your courteous offer. 'Sheart, I was afraid you would
have been in the fashion too, and have remembered to
have forgot your relations. Here's your cousin Tony; 535
belike I mayn't call him brother for fear of offense.

LADY WISHFORT.

Oh, he's a rallier, nephew. My cousin's a wit; and your great
wits always rally their best friends to choose. When you have
been abroad, nephew, you'll understand raillery better.

                    Fainall *and* Mrs. Marwood *talk apart.*

SIR WILFULL.

Why then, let him hold his tongue in the meantime, and 540
rail when that day comes.

                    Enter Mincing.

MINCING.

Mem, I come to acquaint your la'ship that dinner is
impatient.

SIR WILFULL.

Impatient? Why then, belike it won't stay till I pull off my
boots. Sweetheart, can you help me to a pair of slippers? 545
My man's with his horses, I warrant.

LADY WISHFORT.

Fie, fie, nephew, you would not pull off your boots here. Go
down into the hall; dinner shall stay for you. My nephew's
a little unbred; you'll pardon him, madam. Gentlemen,
will you walk? Marwood?   550

---

537. *rallier*] one who indulges in raillery.

538. *rally their best friends to choose*] make as much fun of them as
they like.

MRS. MARWOOD.

I'll follow you, madam, before Sir Wilfull is ready.

Exeunt all but Mrs. Marwood *and* Fainall.

FAINALL.

Why then, Foible's a bawd, an arrant, rank, match-
making bawd. And I, it seems, am a husband, a rank
husband; and my wife a very arrant, rank wife, all in the
way of the world. 'Sdeath, to be an anticipated cuckold, a 555
cuckold in embryo! Sure I was born with budding antlers,
like a young satyr, or a citizen's child. 'Sdeath, to be out-
witted, to be out-jilted, out-matrimonied! If I had kept
my speed like a stag, 'twere somewhat; but to crawl after,
with my horns like a snail, and outstripped by my wife, 'tis 560
scurvy wedlock.

MRS. MARWOOD.

Then shake it off. You have often wished for an opportunity
to part; and now you have it. But first prevent their plot;
the half of Millamant's fortune is too considerable to be
parted with, to a foe, to Mirabell. 565

FAINALL.

Damn him! that had been mine, had you not made that
fond discovery. That had been forfeited, had they been
married. My wife had added luster to my horns by that
increase of fortune; I could have worn 'em tipt with gold,
though my forehead had been furnished like a deputy 570
lieutenant's hall.

MRS. MARWOOD.

They may prove a cap of maintenance to you still, if you
can away with your wife. And she's no worse than when
you had her. I dare swear she had given up her game
before she was married. 575

555. an anticipated cuckold] *Q1; a*   560. and outstripped] *Q1;* and be
cuckold by anticipation *W1.*   outstripped *Q2, W1.*

557. *citizen's child*] Citizens were often cuckolded by fine gentlemen of
the town.

561. *scurvy*] contemptible.   567. *fond*] foolish.

570–571. *deputy lieutenant's hall*] i.e., with numerous antlers.

572. *cap of maintenance*] a technical term in heraldry, implying that
being cuckolded will help to maintain him financially.

573. *away with*] endure.

FAINALL.

Hum! That may be. She might throw up her cards; but I'll be hanged if she did not put Pam in her pocket.

MRS. MARWOOD.

You married her to keep you; and if you can contrive to have her keep you better than you expected, why should you not keep her longer than you intended?   580

FAINALL.

The means, the means.

MRS. MARWOOD.

Discover to my lady your wife's conduct; threaten to part with her. My lady loves her, and will come to any composition to save her reputation. Take the opportunity of breaking it, just upon the discovery of this imposture. My 585 lady will be enraged beyond bounds, and sacrifice niece and fortune and all, at that conjuncture. And let me alone to keep her warm; if she should flag in her part, I will not fail to prompt her.

FAINALL.

Faith, this has an appearance.   590

MRS. MARWOOD.

I'm sorry I hinted to my lady to endeavor a match between Millamant and Sir Wilfull; that may be an obstacle.

FAINALL.

Oh, for that matter leave me to manage him; I'll disable him for that. He will drink like a Dane; after dinner, I'll set his hand in.   595

MRS. MARWOOD.

Well, how do you stand affected towards your lady?

FAINALL.

Why, faith, I'm thinking of it. Let me see. I am married

576–577. She might ... pocket] *Q1;*
omitted in W1.

---

577. *Pam . . . pocket*] Pam, the jack of clubs, is the highest card in the game of loo. Fainall implies that although his wife might have given up other lovers, she has an "ace" up her sleeve, i.e., Mirabell.

583–584. *composition*] agreement.

590. *appearance*] probability (of succeeding).

594. *drink like a Dane*] drink to excess.

594–595. *set his hand in*] start him.

already, so that's over. My wife has played the jade with
me; well, that's over too. I never loved her, or if I had, why
that would have been over too by this time. Jealous of her 600
I cannot be, for I am certain; so there's an end of jealousy.
Weary of her I am, and shall be. No, there's no end of
that; no, no, that were too much to hope. Thus far concerning my repose; now for my reputation. As to my own,
I married not for it; so that's out of the question. And as to 605
my part in my wife's, why she had parted with hers before;
so bringing none to me, she can take none from me. 'Tis
against all rule of play that I should lose to one who has not
wherewithal to stake.

MRS. MARWOOD.

Besides, you forget, marriage is honorable. 610

FAINALL.

Hum! Faith, and that's well thought on. Marriage is
honorable, as you say; and if so, wherefore should cuckol-
dom be a discredit, being derived from so honorable a root?

MRS. MARWOOD.

Nay, I know not; if the root be honorable, why not the
branches? 615

FAINALL.

So, so; why this point's clear. Well, how do we proceed?

MRS. MARWOOD.

I will contrive a letter which shall be delivered to my lady
at the time when that rascal who is to act Sir Rowland is
with her. It shall come as from an unknown hand, for the
less I appear to know of the truth, the better I can play the 620
incendiary. Besides, I would not have Foible provoked if I
could help it, because you know she knows some passages.
Nay, I expect all will come out; but let the mine be sprung
first, and then I care not if I'm discovered.

FAINALL.

If the worst come to the worst, I'll turn my wife to grass. 625
I have already a deed of settlement of the best part of her

---

598. *played the jade*] acted the part of a hussy.
600. *Jealous*] suspicious.
615. *branches*] i.e., of the cuckold's horns.
625. *turn . . . grass*] turn her out to pasture.

estate, which I have wheedled out of her; and that you
shall partake at least.

MRS. MARWOOD.

I hope you are convinced that I hate Mirabell; now you'll
be no more jealous.   630

FAINALL.

Jealous! No, by this kiss. Let husbands be jealous; but let
the lover still believe. Or if he doubt, let it be only to endear
his pleasure, and prepare the joy that follows, when he
proves his mistress true. But let husbands' doubts convert to
endless jealousy; or if they have belief, let it corrupt to super- 635
stition and blind credulity. I am single, and will herd no
more with 'em. True, I wear the badge, but I'll disown the
order. And since I take my leave of 'em, I care not if I leave
'em a common motto to their common crest:

All husbands must or pain or shame endure;   640
The wise too jealous are, fools too secure.   *Exeunt.*

[IV]   *Scene continues.*
                Enter Lady Wishfort *and* Foible.

LADY WISHFORT.

Is Sir Rowland coming, say'st thou, Foible? and are things
in order?

FOIBLE.

Yes, madam, I have put wax lights in the sconces, and
placed the footmen in a row in the hall, in their best liveries,
with the coachman and postilion to fill up the equipage.   5

LADY WISHFORT.

Have you pulvilled the coachman and postilion that they
may not stink of the stable when Sir Rowland comes by?

FOIBLE.

Yes, madam.

LADY WISHFORT.

And are the dancers and the music ready, that he may be
entertained in all points with correspondence to his passion?   10

---

640. *or pain*] either pain.
[IV]
    5. *equipage*] retinue.
    6. *pulvilled*] sprinkled with perfumed powder.

FOIBLE.

All is ready, madam.

LADY WISHFORT.

And—well—and how do I look, Foible?

FOIBLE.

Most killing well, madam.

LADY WISHFORT.

Well, and how shall I receive him? In what figure shall I
give his heart the first impression? There is a great deal in the   15
first impression. Shall I sit? —No, I won't sit—I'll walk—
aye, I'll walk from the door upon his entrance; and then
turn full upon him. —No, that will be too sudden. I'll lie—
aye, I'll lie down—I'll receive him in my little dressing-
room; there's a couch—yes, yes, I'll give the first impression   20
on a couch. —I won't lie neither, but loll and lean upon
one elbow, with one foot a little dangling off, jogging in a
thoughtful way—yes—and then as soon as he appears, start,
aye, start and be surprised, and rise to meet him in a pretty
disorder—yes—oh, nothing is more alluring than a levee   25
from a couch in some confusion. —It shows the foot to
advantage, and furnishes with blushes, and recomposing
airs beyond comparison. Hark! There's a coach.

FOIBLE.

'Tis he, madam.

LADY WISHFORT.

Oh dear, has my nephew made his addresses to Millamant?   30
I ordered him.

FOIBLE.

Sir Wilfull is set in to drinking, madam, in the parlor.

LADY WISHFORT.

Ods my life, I'll send him to her. Call her down, Foible;
bring her hither. I'll send him as I go. When they are
together, then come to me, Foible, that I may not be too long   35
alone with Sir Rowland.   *Exit.*

32. in to] *W1;* into *Q1-2.*

---

25. *levee*] rising.
32. *is set in to*] has set to work at.
33. *Ods my life*] a corruption of *God* [*save*] *my life.*

Enter Mrs. Millamant *and* Mrs. Fainall.

FOIBLE.

Madam, I stayed here, to tell your ladyship that Mr. Mirabell has waited this half hour for an opportunity to talk with you, though my lady's orders were to leave you and Sir Wilfull together. Shall I tell Mr. Mirabell that you are   40 at leisure?

MILLAMANT.

No—what would the dear man have? I am thoughtful and would amuse myself—bid him come another time.

There never yet was woman made,

Nor shall, but to be cursed.   (*Repeating and walking about.*)   45 That's hard!

MRS. FAINALL.

You are very fond of Sir John Suckling today, Millamant, and the poets.

MILLAMANT.

He? Aye, and filthy verses; so I am.

FOIBLE.

Sir Wilfull is coming, madam. Shall I send Mr. Mirabell   50 away?

MILLAMANT.

Aye, if you please, Foible, send him away—or send him hither—just as you will, dear Foible. —I think I'll see him— shall I? Aye, let the wretch come.   [*Exit* Foible.]

Thyrsis, a youth of the inspired train.   (*Repeating.*)   55 Dear Fainall, entertain Sir Wilfull. Thou hast philosophy to undergo a fool; thou art married and hast patience. I would confer with my own thoughts.

MRS. FAINALL.

I am obliged to you, that you would make me your proxy in this affair; but I have business of my own.   60

Enter Sir Wilfull.

O Sir Wilfull, you are come at the critical instant. There's your mistress up to the ears in love and contemplation;

44–45. *There never yet . . . cursed*] the first lines of an untitled poem by Sir John Suckling.

55. *Thyrsis, a youth of the inspired train*] the first line of Edmund Waller's *The Story of Phoebus and Daphne, Applied.*

57. *undergo*] endure.

pursue your point, now or never.

SIR WILFULL.

Yes; my aunt would have it so. I would gladly have been
encouraged with a bottle or two, because I'm somewhat   65
wary at first, before I am acquainted. (*This while* Millamant *walks about repeating to herself.*) But I hope, after a
time, I shall break my mind; that is, upon further acquaintance. So for the present, cousin, I'll take my leave. If so be
you'll be so kind to make my excuse, I'll return to my   70
company.

MRS. FAINALL.

Oh, fie, Sir Wilfull! What, you must not be daunted.

SIR WILFULL.

Daunted! No, that's not it. It is not so much for that; for if
so be that I set on't, I'll do't. But only for the present; 'tis
sufficient till further acquaintance, that's all. Your servant.   75

MRS. FAINALL.

Nay, I'll swear you shall never lose so favorable an opportunity, if I can help it. I'll leave you together and lock the
door.   *Exit.*

SIR WILFULL.

Nay, nay, cousin. I have forgot my gloves. What d'ye do?
'Sheart, 'a has locked the door indeed, I think. Nay, Cousin   80
Fainall, open the door! Pshaw, what a vixen trick is this?
Nay, now 'a has seen me too. Cousin, I made bold to pass
through as it were. I think this door's enchanted!

MILLAMANT (*repeating*).

I prithee spare me, gentle boy,
Press me no more for that slight toy—   85

SIR WILFULL.

Anan? Cousin, your servant.

MILLAMANT (*repeating*).

That foolish trifle of a heart—
Sir Wilfull!

64. would have] *Q1;* will have *Q2,*
W1.

---

80. *'a*] a countrified abbreviation of *she* (more commonly *he*).

84–85. *I prithee . . . toy*] These two lines and the three which Millamant
next repeats constitute the first stanza of an untitled poem by Suckling.

86. *Anan?*] a countrified expression meaning *What?* or *What say?*

SIR WILFULL.

Yes. Your servant. No offense, I hope, cousin.

MILLAMANT (*repeating*).

I swear it will not do its part,   90
Though thou dost thine, employ'st thy power and art.
Natural, easy Suckling!

SIR WILFULL.

Anan? Suckling? No such suckling neither, cousin, nor
stripling; I thank heaven, I'm no minor.

MILLAMANT.

Ah, rustic! ruder than Gothic!   95

SIR WILFULL.

Well, well, I shall understand your lingo one of these days,
cousin; in the meanwhile, I must answer in plain English.

MILLAMANT.

Have you any business with me, Sir Wilfull?

SIR WILFULL.

Not at present, cousin. Yes, I made bold to see, to come and
know if that how you were disposed to fetch a walk this 100
evening, if so be that I might not be troublesome, I would
have fought a walk with you.

MILLAMANT.

A walk! What then?

SIR WILFULL.

Nay, nothing. Only for the walk's sake, that's all.

MILLAMANT.

I nauseate walking; 'tis a country diversion. I loathe the 105
country and everything that relates to it.

SIR WILFULL.

Indeed! Ha! Look ye, look ye, you do? Nay, 'tis like you
may. Here are choice of pastimes here in town, as plays and
the like; that must be confessed indeed.

MILLAMANT.

Ah, *l'étourdie!* I hate the town too.   110

102. fought] *Q1–2;* sought *W1.*

---

95. *Gothic*] barbarian.
102. *fought*] a provincial form of *fetched*.
110. *Ah, l'étourdie!*] Ah, the giddy town! Some editors have emended to
Ah, l'étourdi, meaning *Ah, the dolt!*

SIR WILFULL.

Dear heart, that's much. Ha! that you should hate 'em both!
Ha! 'tis like you may; there are some can't relish the town,
and others can't away with the country. 'Tis like you may
be one of those, cousin.

MILLAMANT.

Ha! ha! ha! Yes, 'tis like I may. You have nothing further 115
to say to me?

SIR WILFULL.

Not at present, cousin. 'Tis like when I have an opportunity
to be more private, I may break my mind in some measure.
I conjecture you partly guess. —However, that's as time shall
try; but spare to speak and spare to speed, as they say.   120

MILLAMANT.

If it is of no great importance, Sir Wilfull, you will oblige
me to leave me; I have just now a little business—

SIR WILFULL.

Enough, enough, cousin, yes, yes, all a case; when you're
disposed, when you're disposed. Now's as well as another
time; and another time as well as now. All's one for that. 125
Yes, yes, if your concerns call you, there's no haste; it will
keep cold, as they say. Cousin, your servant. I think this
door's locked.

MILLAMANT.

You may go this way, sir.

SIR WILFULL.

Your servant; then with your leave I'll return to my 130
company.   *Exit.*

MILLAMANT.

Aye, aye; ha! ha! ha!
Like Phoebus sung the no less amorous boy.

Enter Mirabell.

MIRABELL.

Like Daphne she, as lovely and as coy.
Do you lock yourself up from me, to make my search more 135

---

123. *all a case*] all the same.
133. *Like Phoebus sung the no less amorous boy*] the third line of the poem
by Waller previously quoted by Millamant. Mirabell, entering, completes
the couplet.

curious? Or is this pretty artifice contrived, to signify that here the chase must end and my pursuit be crowned, for you can fly no further?

MILLAMANT.

Vanity! No. I'll fly and be followed to the last moment. Though I am upon the very verge of matrimony, I expect 140 you should solicit me as much as if I were wavering at the grate of a monastery, with one foot over the threshold. I'll be solicited to the very last, nay and afterwards.

MIRABELL.

What, after the last?

MILLAMANT.

Oh, I should think I was poor and had nothing to bestow, 145 if I were reduced to an inglorious ease and freed from the agreeable fatigues of solicitation.

MIRABELL.

But do not you know that when favors are conferred upon instant and tedious solicitation, that they diminish in their value, and that both the giver loses the grace, and the 150 receiver lessens his pleasure?

MILLAMANT.

It may be in things of common application; but never sure in love. Oh, I hate a lover that can dare to think he draws a moment's air independent on the bounty of his mistress. There is not so impudent a thing in nature as the saucy look 155 of an assured man, confident of success. The pedantic arrogance of a very husband has not so pragmatical an air. Ah! I'll never marry, unless I am first made sure of my will and pleasure.

MIRABELL.

Would you have 'em both before marriage? Or will you be 160 contented with the first now, and stay for the other till after grace?

MILLAMANT.

Ah! don't be impertinent. —My dear liberty, shall I leave

---

136. *curious*] complicated.
152. *things of common application*] affairs of everyday life.
157. *pragmatical*] matter-of-fact.
161–162. *after grace*] referring to the prayer concluding the marriage ceremony.

thee? My faithful solitude, my darling contemplation, must
I bid you then adieu? Ay-h adieu—my morning thoughts, 165
agreeable wakings, indolent slumbers, all ye *douceurs*, ye
sommeils du matin, adieu? —I can't do't, 'tis more than
impossible. Positively, Mirabell, I'll lie abed in a morning as
long as I please.

MIRABELL.

Then I'll get up in a morning as early as I please.   170

MILLAMANT.

Ah! Idle creature, get up when you will. —And d'ye hear,
I won't be called names after I'm married; positively I won't
be called names.

MIRABELL.

Names!

MILLAMANT.

Aye, as wife, spouse, my dear, joy, jewel, love, sweetheart, 175
and the rest of that nauseous cant, in which men and their
wives are so fulsomely familiar—I shall never bear that.
—Good Mirabell, don't let us be familiar or fond, nor kiss
before folks, like my Lady Fadler and Sir Francis; nor go
to Hyde Park together the first Sunday in a new chariot, to 180
provoke eyes and whispers; and then never to be seen there
together again; as if we were proud of one another the
first week, and ashamed of one another ever after. Let us
never visit together, nor go to a play together. But let us be
very strange and well-bred; let us be as strange as if we had 185
been married a great while, and as well-bred as if we were
not married at all.

MIRABELL.

Have you any more conditions to offer? Hitherto your
demands are pretty reasonable.

MILLAMANT.

Trifles! —As liberty to pay and receive visits to and from 190
whom I please; to write and receive letters, without interro-

181. never to be] *Q1;* never be   183. ever after] *Q2, W1;* for ever
W1.   after *Q1.*

---

166. *douceurs*] sweetnesses.
167. *sommeils du matin*] morning slumbers.
179. *Fadler*] To faddle is to fondle.   185. *strange*] reserved.

gatories or wry faces on your part; to wear what I please; and choose conversation with regard only to my own taste; to have no obligation upon me to converse with wits that I don't like, because they are your acquaintance; or to be 195 intimate with fools, because they may be your relations. Come to dinner when I please; dine in my dressing room when I'm out of humor, without giving a reason. To have my closet inviolate; to be sole empress of my tea table, which you must never presume to approach without first asking 200 leave. And lastly, wherever I am, you shall always knock at the door before you come in. These articles subscribed, if I continue to endure you a little longer, I may by degrees dwindle into a wife.

MIRABELL.

Your bill of fare is something advanced in this latter 205 account. Well, have I liberty to offer conditions—that when you are dwindled into a wife, I may not be beyond measure enlarged into a husband?

MILLAMANT.

You have free leave. Propose your utmost; speak and spare not. 210

MIRABELL.

I thank you. *Imprimis* then, I covenant that your acquaintance be general; that you admit no sworn confidante, or intimate of your own sex; no she-friend to screen her affairs under your countenance, and tempt you to make trial of a mutual secrecy. No decoy-duck to wheedle you a fop, 215 scrambling to the play in a mask; then bring you home in a pretended fright, when you think you shall be found out, and rail at me for missing the play, and disappointing the frolic which you had, to pick me up and prove my constancy.

MILLAMANT.

Detestable *imprimis!* I go to the play in a mask! 220

MIRABELL.

Item, I article that you continue to like your own face as

---

211. *Imprimis*] In the first place.
215-216. *decoy-duck . . . mask*] a female confidante to coax a fop to hurry you, masked, to the theater.
221. *article*] stipulate.

long as I shall; and while it passes current with me, that
you endeavor not to new-coin it. To which end, together
with all vizards for the day, I prohibit all masks for the
night, made of oiled skins and I know now what—hog's   225
bones, hare's gall, pig-water, and the marrow of a roasted
cat. In short, I forbid all commerce with the gentlewoman in
What-d'ye-call-it Court. *Item*, I shut my doors against all
bawds with baskets, and pennyworths of muslin, china,
fans, atlases, etc. —*Item*, when you shall be breeding—   230

MILLAMANT.

Ah! name it not.

MIRABELL.

Which may be presumed, with a blessing on our endeavors—

MILLAMANT.

Odious endeavors!

MIRABELL.

I denounce against all strait-lacing, squeezing for a shape, 235
till you mold my boy's head like a sugar loaf, and instead
of a man-child, make me the father to a crooked billet.
Lastly, to the dominion of the tea table I submit, but with
proviso, that you exceed not in your province, but restrain
yourself to native and simple tea-table drinks, as tea,   240
chocolate, and coffee. As likewise to genuine and authorized
tea-table talk—such as mending of fashions, spoiling reputations, railing at absent friends, and so forth; but that on
no account you encroach upon the men's prerogative, and
presume to drink healths, or toast fellows; for prevention of 245
which, I banish all foreign forces, all auxiliaries to the tea
table, as orange brandy, all aniseed, cinnamon, citron, and
Barbadoes waters, together with ratafia and the most

227. gentlewoman] *Q1, W1;* gentle-   237. me the father] *Q1;* me father
women *Q2.*   *W1.*

---

224. *vizards*] masks.
226. *pig-water*] an ingredient in cosmetics.
227–228. *gentlewoman in What-d'ye-call-it Court*] referring to a seller of
cosmetics.
230. *atlases*] a kind of oriental satin.
237. *billet*] small stick.
248. *Barbadoes waters*] brandy flavored with orange and lemon peel.

noble spirit of clary. But for cowslip-wine, poppy-water, and all dormitives, those I allow. These provisos admitted, in other things I may prove a tractable and complying husband.   250

MILLAMANT.

Oh, horrid provisos! filthy strong waters! I toast fellows, odious men! I hate your odious provisos.

MIRABELL.

Then we're agreed. Shall I kiss your hand upon the contract? And here comes one to be a witness to the sealing of the deed.   255

Enter Mrs. Fainall.

MILLAMANT.

Fainall, what shall I do? Shall I have him? I think I must have him.

MRS. FAINALL.

Aye, aye, take him, take him, what should you do?   260

MILLAMANT.

Well then—I'll take my death I'm in a horrid fright— Fainall, I shall never say it—well—I think—I'll endure you.

MRS. FAINALL.

Fie, fie! have him, have him, and tell him so in plain terms; for I am sure you have a mind to him.

MILLAMANT.

Are you? I think I have—and the horrid man looks as if he thought so too. —Well, you ridiculous thing you, I'll have you—I won't be kissed, nor I won't be thanked—here, kiss my hand though. —So, hold your tongue now, and don't say a word.   265

MRS FAINALL.

Mirabell, there's a necessity for your obedience; you have neither time to talk nor stay. My mother is coming; and in my conscience, if she should see you, would fall into fits and maybe not recover, time enough to return to Sir Rowland,   270

---

268. and don't] *Q1;* and *omitted in*
W1.

---

249. *clary*] clary water, brandy flavored with clary flowers and various spices.
250. *dormitives*] drinks to promote sleep.

who, as Foible tells me, is in a fair way to succeed. Therefore
spare your ecstasies for another occasion, and slip down the 275
backstairs, where Foible waits to consult you.

MILLAMANT.

Aye, go, go. In the meantime I suppose you have said
something to please me.

MIRABELL.

I am all obedience.   *Exit.*

MRS. FAINALL.

Yonder Sir Wilfull's drunk, and so noisy that my mother 280
has been forced to leave Sir Rowland to appease him; but
he answers her only with singing and drinking. What they
have done by this time I know not; but Petulant and he
were quarreling as I came by.

MILLAMANT.

Well, if Mirabell should not make a good husband, I am a 285
lost thing—for I find I love him violently.

MRS. FAINALL.

So it seems, when you mind not what's said to you. If you
doubt him, you had best take up with Sir Wilfull.

MILLAMANT.

How can you name that superannuated lubber? foh!

Enter Witwoud *from drinking*.

MRS. FAINALL.

So, is the fray made up, that you have left 'em?   290

WITWOUD.

Left 'em? I could stay no longer. I have laughed like ten
christenings; I am tipsy with laughing. If I had stayed any
longer I should have burst; I must have been let out and
pieced in the sides like an unsized camlet. Yes, yes, the fray
is composed; my lady came in like a *nolle prosequi* and stopped 295
their proceedings.

282–283. they have] *Q1;* they may   *Q1–2, W1.*
have *W1.*   296. their proceedings] *Q1;* the
295. *nolle prosequi*] *Spelled noli prosequi*   proceedings *W1.*

---

294. *unsized camlet*] an unstiffened oriental fabric.
295. *nolle prosequi*] a legal term for terminating the prosecution of a
lawsuit.

MILLAMANT.

What was the dispute?

WITWOUD.

That's the jest; there was no dispute. They could neither of
'em speak for rage, and so fell a-sputtering at one another
like two roasting apples.   300

Enter Petulant *drunk.*

Now Petulant, all's over, all's well. Gad, my head begins
to whim it about. Why dost thou not speak? Thou art both
as drunk and as mute as a fish.

PETULANT.

Look you, Mrs. Millamant, if you can love me, dear nymph,
say it, and that's the conclusion. Pass on, or pass off; that's   305
all.

WITWOUD.

Thou hast uttered volumes, folios, in less than *decimo sexto*,
my dear Lacedemonian. Sirrah Petulant, thou art an epitomizer of words.

PETULANT.

Witwoud, you are an annihilator of sense.   310

WITWOUD.

Thou art a retailer of phrases and dost deal in remnants
of remnants, like a maker of pincushions; thou art in truth
(metaphorically speaking) a speaker of shorthand.

PETULANT.

Thou art (without a figure) just one half of an ass, and
Baldwin yonder, thy half brother, is the rest. A gemini of   315
asses split would make just four of you.

WITWOUD.

Thou dost bite, my dear mustard seed; kiss me for that.

---

302. *whim it about*] spin.

307. *decimo sexto*] a small-sized book in which each sheet is folded
into sixteen leaves.

308. *Lacedemonian*] Spartan. The Spartans were famous for brevity of
speech.

308–309. *epitomizer*] one who states briefly the essence of a matter.

315. *Baldwin*] the name of the ass in the beast epic of Reynard the Fox.

315. *gemini*] a pair of twins.

317. *mustard seed*] A paste made from mustard seeds, with the addition
of water and vinegar, was a pungent kind of seasoning.

PETULANT.

> Stand off! I'll kiss no more males. I have kissed your twin
> yonder in a humor of reconciliation, till he   (*hiccup*)   rises
> upon my stomach like a radish.   320

MILLAMANT.

> Eh! filthy creature! What was the quarrel?

PETULANT.

> There was no quarrel; there might have been a quarrel.

WITWOUD.

> If there had been words enow between 'em to have ex-
> pressed provocation, they had gone together by the ears
> like a pair of castanets.   325

PETULANT.

> You were the quarrel.

MILLAMANT.

> Me!

PETULANT.

> If I have a humor to quarrel, I can make less matters
> conclude premises. If you are not handsome, what then,
> if I have a humor to prove it? If I shall have my reward, 330
> say so; if not, fight for your face the next time yourself.
> I'll go sleep.

WITWOUD.

> Do, wrap thyself up like a wood louse, and dream revenge;
> and hear me, if thou canst learn to write by tomorrow
> morning, pen me a challenge. I'll carry it for thee.   335

PETULANT.

> Carry your mistress's monkey a spider! Go flea dogs, and
> read romances! I'll go to bed to my maid.   *Exit.*

MRS. FAINALL.

> He's horridly drunk. How came you all in this pickle?

WITWOUD.

> A plot! a plot! to get rid of the knight. Your husband's
> advice; but he sneaked off.   340

---

323. *enow*] enough.

329. *conclude premises*] bring matters to a head.

333. *wood louse*] small insect found in old wood or under stones, capable
of rolling itself up in a ball.

336. *flea dogs*] pick fleas from the coats of lap-dogs.

Enter Lady Wishfort, *and* Sir Wilfull *drunk.*

LADY WISHFORT.

Out upon't, out upon't! At years of discretion, and comport yourself at this rantipole rate!

SIR WILFULL.

No offense, aunt.

LADY WISHFORT.

Offense? As I'm a person, I'm ashamed of you—foh! how you stink of wine! D'ye think my niece will ever endure 345 such a borachio! you're an absolute borachio.

SIR WILFULL.

Borachio!

LADY WISHFORT.

At a time when you should commence an amour and put your best foot foremost—

SIR WILFULL.

'Sheart, an you grutch me your liquor, make a bill. Give me 350 more drink, and take my purse.   *Sings.*

Prithee fill me the glass,
Till it laugh in my face,
With ale that is potent and mellow;
He that whines for a lass   355
Is an ignorant ass,
For a bumper has not its fellow.

But if you would have me marry my cousin, say the word, and I'll do't. Wilfull will do't; that's the word. Wilfull will do't; that's my crest. My motto I have forgot.   360

LADY WISHFORT.

My nephew's a little overtaken, cousin, but 'tis with drinking your health. O' my word you are obliged to him.

SIR WILFULL.

In vino veritas, aunt. If I drunk your health today, cousin,

353. laugh] *Q1, W1;* laughs *Q2.*

---

342. *rantipole*] ill-mannered.   344. *foh!*] an exclamation of disgust.
346. *borachio*] drunkard. The term is derived from the Spanish word for winebag.
350. *grutch*] grudge.   361. *overtaken*] overcome.
363. *In vino veritas*] In wine there is truth, i.e., drunkards frankly speak the truth.

I am a borachio. But if you have a mind to be married, say
the word, and send for the piper; Wilfull will do't. If not, 365
dust it away, and let's have t'other round. —Tony! —Ods-
heart, where's Tony? —Tony's an honest fellow; but he
spits after a bumper, and that's a fault.   *Sings.*

    We'll drink, and we'll never ha' done, boys,
    Put the glass then around with the sun, boys;   370
  Let Apollo's example invite us;
    For he's drunk every night,
    And that makes him so bright,
  That he's able next morning to light us.

The sun's a good pimple, an honest soaker; he has a cellar 375
at your Antipodes. If I travel, aunt, I touch at your Antipodes; your Antipodes are a good, rascally sort of topsy-
turvy fellows. If I had a bumper, I'd stand upon my head
and drink a health to 'em. A match, or no match, cousin with
the hard name? Aunt, Wilfull will do't. If she has her 380
maidenhead, let her look to't; if she has not, let her keep
her own counsel in the meantime, and cry out at the nine
months' end.

MILLAMANT.

Your pardon, madam, I can stay no longer. Sir Wilfull
grows very powerful. Egh! how he smells! I shall be over- 385
come if I stay. Come, cousin.

               Exeunt Millamant *and* Mrs. Fainall.

LADY WISHFORT.

Smells! he would poison a tallow chandler and his family.
Beastly creature, I know not what to do with him! Travel,
quotha! aye, travel, travel, get thee gone, get thee but far
enough, to the Saracens, or the Tartars, or the Turks, for 390
thou art not fit to live in a Christian commonwealth, thou
beastly pagan!

SIR WILFULL.

Turks, no; no Turks, aunt; your Turks are infidels, and
believe not in the grape. Your Mahometan, your Mussul-
man, is a dry stinkard. No offense, aunt. My map says that 395

---

375. *pimple*] boon companion.
376. *Antipodes*] the opposite side of the earth and its inhabitants.
387. *tallow chandler*] a maker or seller of tallow candles.
395. *dry stinkard*] a stinking non-drinker.

your Turk is not so honest a man as your Christian. I
cannot find by the map that your Mufti is orthodox; whereby it is a plain case that orthodox is a hard word, aunt,
and   (*hiccup*) Greek for claret.   *Sings.*

   To drink is a Christian diversion,   400
   Unknown to the Turk and the Persian:
      Let Mahometan fools
      Live by heathenish rules,
  And. be damned over tea cups and coffee!
      But let British lads sing,   405
      Crown a health to the king,
  And a fig for your sultan and sophy!
Ah, Tony!

Enter Foible, *and whispers* Lady Wishfort.

LADY WISHFORT [*aside to* Foible].
   Sir Rowland impatient? Good lack! what shall I do with this
   beastly tumbril? [*Aloud.*] Go lie down and sleep, you 410
   sot! or, as I'm a person, I'll have you bastinadoed with
   broomsticks. Call up the wenches.   *Exit* Foible.

SIR WILFULL.
   Ahey! Wenches, where are the wenches?

LADY WISHFORT.
   Dear Cousin Witwoud, get him away, and you will bind
   me to you inviolably. I have an affair of moment that 415
   invades me with some precipitation. You will oblige me to
   all futurity.

WITWOUD.
   Come, knight. Pox on him, I don't know what to say to
   him. Will you go to a cock-match?

SIR WILFULL.
   With a wench, Tony? Is she a shake-bag, Sirrah? Let me 420

401. Turk and] *Q1;* Turk or *W1.*   with broomsticks *W1.*
412. the wenches] *Q1;* the wenches

---

  397. *Mufti*] Mohammedan priest.
  407. *sophy*] the Shah of Persia.   410. *tumbril*] heavy cart.
  411. *bastinadoed*] beaten on the soles of the feet.
  420. *shake-bag*] large gamecock.

bite your cheek for that.

WITWOUD.

Horrible! He has a breath like a bagpipe! Aye, aye, come,
will you march, my Salopian?

SIR WILFULL.

Lead on, little Tony; I'll follow thee, my Anthony, my
Tantony. Sirrah, thou shalt be my Tantony, and I'll be thy 425
pig.

And a fig for your sultan and sophy.

Exit singing with Witwoud.

LADY WISHFORT.

This will never do. It will never make a match—at least
before he has been abroad.

Enter Waitwell, *disguised as for* Sir Rowland.

Dear Sir Rowland, I am confounded with confusion at the 430
retrospection of my own rudeness! I have more pardons to
ask than the Pope distributes in the Year of Jubilee. But I
hope, where there is likely to be so near an alliance, we
may unbend the severity of decorum and dispense with a
little ceremony.   435

WAITWELL.

My impatience, madam, is the effect of my transport;
and till I have the possession of your adorable person, I am
tantalized on a rack, and do but hang, madam, on the
tenter of expectation.

LADY WISHFORT.

You have an excess of gallantry, Sir Rowland, and press 440
things to a conclusion with a most prevailing vehemence.
But a day or two for decency of marriage—

WAITWELL.

For decency of funeral, madam! The delay will break

438. a rack] *Q1;* the rack *Q2, W1.*

---

423. *Salopian*] native of Shropshire.

425. *Tantony*] a corruption of St. Anthony, renowned for his triumph
over gluttony. He was commonly represented in art as followed by a pig.

431. *retrospection*] act of looking back on the past.

432. *Year of Jubilee*] the year in which the Pope proclaims remission of
the punishment imposed for sin. The year in which this play was first
acted (1700) was a jubilee year.

439. *tenter*] tenterhook.

my heart; or, if that should fail, I shall be poisoned. My
nephew will get an inkling of my designs and poison me; 445
and I would willingly starve him before I die; I would
gladly go out of the world with that satisfaction. That
would be some comfort to me, if I could but live so long as
to be revenged on that unnatural viper.

LADY WISHFORT.

Is he so unnatural, say you? Truly I would contribute much 450
both to the saving of your life, and the accomplishment of
your revenge. Not that I respect myself, though he has been
a perfidious wretch to me.

WAITWELL.

Perfidious to you!

LADY WISHFORT.

O Sir Rowland, the hours that he has died away at my feet, 455
the tears that he has shed, the oaths that he has sworn, the
palpitations that he has felt, the trances and the tremblings,
the ardors and the ecstasies, the kneelings and the risings,
the heart-heavings, and the hand-grippings, the pangs and
the pathetic regards of his protesting eyes! Oh, no memory 460
can register.

WAITWELL.

What, my rival! Is the rebel my rival? 'A dies.

LADY WISHFORT.

No, don't kill him at once, Sir Rowland; starve him
gradually, inch by inch.

WAITWELL.

I'll do't. In three weeks he shall be barefoot; in a month 465
out at knees with begging an alms. He shall starve upward
and upward, till he has nothing living but his head, and
then go out in a stink like a candle's end upon a save-all.

LADY WISHFORT.

Well, Sir Rowland, you have the way. You are no novice in
the labyrinth of love; you have the clue. But as I am a person, 470
Sir Rowland, you must not attribute my yielding to any
sinister appetite, or indigestion of widowhood; nor impute

---

452. *respect*] consider.
468. *save-all*] a device in a candlestick to hold the ends of candles so
that they may be burned.

my complacency to any lethargy of continence. I hope you
do not think me prone to any iteration of nuptials.

WAITWELL.

Far be it from me—   475

LADY WISHFORT.

If you do, I protest I must recede, or think that I have
made a prostitution of decorums; but in the vehemence of
compassion, and to save the life of a person of so much
importance—

WAITWELL.

I esteem it so.   480

LADY WISHFORT.

Or else you wrong my condescension.

WAITWELL.

I do not, I do not!

LADY WISHFORT.

Indeed you do.

WAITWELL.

I do not, fair shrine of virtue!

LADY WISHFORT.

If you think the least scruple of carnality was an ingredient— 485

WAITWELL.

Dear madam, no. You are all camphire and frankincense,
all chastity and odor.

LADY WISHFORT.

Or that—

Enter Foible.

FOIBLE.

Madam, the dancers are ready, and there's one with a
letter, who must deliver it into your own hands.   490

LADY WISHFORT.

Sir Rowland, will you give me leave? Think favorably,
judge candidly, and conclude you have found a person who
would suffer racks in honor's cause, dear Sir Rowland, and
will wait on you incessantly.   *Exit.*

WAITWELL.

Fie, fie! What a slavery have I undergone! Spouse, hast 495

---

486. *camphire*] camphor, supposed to lessen sexual desire.
494. *incessantly*] instantly.

thou any cordial? I want spirits.

FOIBLE.

What a washy rogue art thou, to pant thus for a quarter of
an hour's lying and swearing to a fine lady!

WAITWELL.

Oh, she is the antidote to desire! Spouse, thou wilt fare the
worse for't. I shall have no appetite to iteration of nuptials 500
this eight-and-forty hours. By this hand I'd rather be a
chairman in the dog-days than act Sir Rowland till this
time tomorrow!

Enter Lady Wishfort, *with a letter.*

LADY WISHFORT.

Call in the dancers. Sir Rowland, we'll sit, if you please,
and see the entertainment.   505

Dance.

Now, with your permission, Sir Rowland, I will peruse my
letter. I would open it in your presence, because I would
not make you uneasy. If it should make you uneasy, I would
burn it. Speak, if it does. But you may see by the superscription it is like a woman's hand.   510

FOIBLE [*aside to* Waitwell].

By heaven! Mrs. Marwood's; I know it. My heart aches.
Get it from her.

WAITWELL.

A woman's hand? No, madam, that's no woman's hand;
I see that already. That's somebody whose throat must be
cut.   515

LADY WISHFORT.

Nay, Sir Rowland, since you give me a proof of your
passion by your jealousy, I promise you I'll make you a
return, by a frank communication. You shall see it; we'll
open it together. Look you here. (*Reads.*) "Madam,
though unknown to you"—Look you there, 'tis from nobody 520

---

500. iteration] *W1;* interation *Q1–*
2.

509–510. by the superscription it is]
Q1; the superscription is *W1.*

---

497. *washy*] watery.
502. *chairman in the dog-days*] bearer of a sedan chair in the hottest part
of the summer.

that I know—"I have that honor for your character, that I think myself obliged to let you know you are abused. He who pretends to be Sir Rowland is a cheat and a rascal." —Oh, heavens! what's this?

FOIBLE [*aside*].

Unfortunate! all's ruined!   525

WAITWELL.

How, how, let me see, let me see! (*Reading.*) "A rascal, and disguised and suborned for that imposture." —O villainy! O villainy —"by the contrivance of —"

LADY WISHFORT.

I shall faint, I shall die, I shall die, oh!

FOIBLE [*aside to* Waitwell].

Say 'tis your nephew's hand. Quickly, his plot, swear, 530 swear it!

WAITWELL.

Here's a villain! Madam, don't you perceive it? don't you see it?

LADY WISHFORT.

Too well, too well! I have seen too much.

WAITWELL.

I told you at first I knew the hand. A woman's hand? The 535 rascal writes a sort of a large hand, your Roman hand. I saw there was a throat to be cut presently. If he were my son, as he is my nephew, I'd pistol him!

FOIBLE.

Oh, treachery! But are you sure, Sir Rowland, it is his writing?   540

WAITWELL.

Sure? Am I here? Do I live? Do I love this pearl of India? I have twenty letters in my pocket from him in the same character.

LADY WISHFORT.

How!

---

529. I shall faint, I shall die, I shall   die, oh! *Q2, W1.*
die, oh!] *Q1;* I shall faint, I shall

---

536. *Roman hand*] round and bold handwriting.
543. *character*] handwriting.

FOIBLE.

Oh, what luck it is, Sir Rowland, that you were present at 545
this juncture! This was the business that brought Mr.
Mirabell disguised to Madam Millamant this afternoon.
I thought something was contriving, when he stole by me
and would have hid his face.

LADY WISHFORT.

How, how! I heard the villain was in the house indeed; 550
and now I remember, my niece went away abruptly, when
Sir Wilfull was to have made his addresses.

FOIBLE.

Then, then, madam, Mr. Mirabell waited for her in her
chamber, but I would not tell your ladyship to discompose
you when you were to receive Sir Rowland.   555

WAITWELL.

Enough, his date is short.

FOIBLE.

No, good Sir Rowland, don't incur the law.

WAITWELL.

Law? I care not for law. I can but die, and 'tis in a good
cause. My lady shall be satisfied of my truth and innocence,
though it cost me my life.   560

LADY WISHFORT.

No, dear Sir Rowland, don't fight; if you should be killed, I
must never show my face; or hanged—oh, consider my
reputation, Sir Rowland! No, you shan't fight. I'll go in and
examine my niece; I'll make her confess. I conjure you,
Sir Rowland, by all your love, not to fight.   565

WAITWELL.

I am charmed, madam; I obey. But some proof you must
let me give you; I'll go for a black box, which contains the
writings of my whole estate, and deliver that into your hands.

LADY WISHFORT.

Aye, dear Sir Rowland, that will be some comfort; bring the
black box.   570

WAITWELL.

And may I presume to bring a contract to be signed this
night? May I hope so far?

LADY WISHFORT.

Bring what you will; but come alive, pray come alive. Oh,

this is a happy discovery!

WAITWELL.

Dead or alive I'll come, and married we will be in spite of 575
treachery; aye, and get an heir that shall defeat the last
remaining glimpse of hope in my abandoned nephew.
Come, my buxom widow.

    Ere long you shall substantial proof receive
    That I'm an arrant knight—

FOIBLE [aside].   Or arrant knave. *Exeunt.* 580

[V]   *Scene continues.*
    Enter Lady Wishfort *and* Foible.

LADY WISHFORT.

Out of my house, out of my house, thou viper! thou serpent,
that I have fostered! thou bosom traitress that I raised
from nothing! Begone! begone! begone! go! go! That I
took from washing of old gauze and weaving of dead hair,
with a bleak blue nose, over a chafing dish of starved embers, 5
and dining behind a traverse rag, in a shop no bigger than a
birdcage! Go, go! starve again, do, do!

FOIBLE.

Dear madam, I'll beg pardon on my knees.

LADY WISHFORT.

Away! out! out! Go set up for yourself again! Do, drive a
trade, do, with your three-pennyworth of small ware, 10
flaunting upon a pack-thread, under a brandy-seller's bulk,
or against a dead wall by a ballad-monger! Go, hang out an
old frisoneer gorget, with a yard of yellow colberteen again.
Do! an old gnawed mask, two rows of pins, and a child's
fiddle; a glass necklace with the beads broken, and a 15

---

578. *buxom*] gay (the archaic meaning).
580. *arrant knight*] wandering knight.
580. *arrant knave*] downright knave. Foible plays on the word *arrant*
(*errant*), using it in its later sense.
[V]
4. *weaving of dead hair*] i.e., making wigs.
6. *traverse rag*] tattered curtain.
11. *bulk*] stall.
13. *frisoneer gorget*] woollen neckpiece or kerchief.
13. *colberteen*] a kind of cheap lace.

quilted nightcap with one ear. Go, go, drive a trade! These
were your commodities, you treacherous trull! This was your
merchandise you dealt in, when I took you into my house,
placed you next myself, and made you governante of my
whole family! You have forgot this, have you, now you have   20
feathered your nest?

FOIBLE.

No, no, dear madam. Do but hear me; have but a moment's
patience. I'll confess all. Mr. Mirabell seduced me; I am
not the first that he has wheedled with his dissembling
tongue. Your ladyship's own wisdom has been deluded by   25
him; then how should I, a poor ignorant, defend myself?
O madam, if you knew but what he promised me, and how
he assured me your ladyship should come to no damage!
Or else the wealth of the Indies should not have bribed me
to conspire against so good, so sweet, so kind a lady as you   30
have been to me.

LADY WISHFORT.

No damage? What, to betray me, to marry me to a cast
servingman? to make me a receptacle, an hospital for a decayed pimp? No damage? O thou frontless impudence,
more than a big-bellied actress.   35

FOIBLE.

Pray do but hear me, madam; he could not marry your
ladyship, madam. No indeed; his marriage was to have been
void in law, for he was married to me first, to secure your
ladyship. He could not have bedded your ladyship; for if he
had consummated with your ladyship, he must have run   40
the risk of the law and been put upon his clergy. Yes
indeed; I inquired of the law in that case before I would
meddle or make.

17–18. your merchandise] *Q1;* the
merchandise *W1.*

---

19. *governante*] housekeeper.
32–33. *cast servingman*] discharged servant.
34. *frontless*] shameless.
41. *put upon his clergy*] A criminal who could read and write might
escape sentence of death by claiming "benefit of clergy," a privilege origin-
ally restricted to clergymen.
43. *meddle or make*] have anything to do with the affair.

LADY WISHFORT.

What, then I have been your property, have I? I have been
convenient to you, it seems! While you were catering for   45
Mirabell, I have been broker for you? What, have you made
a passive bawd of me? This exceeds all precedent; I am
brought to fine uses, to become a botcher of secondhand
marriages between Abigails and Andrews! I'll couple you!
Yes, I'll baste you together, you and your Philander! I'll   50
Duke's Place you, as I'm a person! Your turtle is in custody
already; you shall coo in the same cage, if there be constable
or warrant in the parish.   *Exit.*

FOIBLE.

Oh, that ever I was born! Oh, that I was ever married!
A bride! aye, I shall be a Bridewell-bride. Oh!   55

Enter Mrs. Fainall.

MRS. FAINALL.

Poor Foible, what's the matter?

FOIBLE.

O madam, my lady's gone for a constable. I shall be had
to a justice, and put to Bridewell to beat hemp. Poor
Waitwell's gone to prison already.

MRS. FAINALL.

Have a good heart, Foible; Mirabell's gone to give   60
security for him. This is all Marwood's and my husband's
doing.

FOIBLE.

Yes, yes, I know it, madam; she was in my lady's closet, and
overheard all that you said to me before dinner. She sent
the letter to my lady; and that missing effect, Mr. Fainall   65
laid this plot to arrest Waitwell, when he pretended to go
for the papers; and in the meantime Mrs. Marwood de-
clared all to my lady.

---

46. *broker*] i.e., marriage broker.

49. *Abigails and Andrews*] waiting maids and menservants.

50. *Philander*] lover.

51. *Duke's Place you*] marry you in a hurry, as at St. James's Church
in Duke's Place, notorious for irregular marriages.

55. *Bridewell-bride*] a bride in Bridewell Prison, where women offenders
were often punished by being required to beat hemp.

MRS. FAINALL.

Was there no mention made of me in the letter? My mother does not suspect my being in the confederacy? I 70 fancy Marwood has not told her, though she has told my husband.

FOIBLE.

Yes, madam; but my lady did not see that part. We stifled the letter before she read so far. Has that mischievous devil told Mr. Fainall of your ladyship then? 75

MRS. FAINALL.

Aye, all's out, my affair with Mirabell, everything discovered. This is the last day of our living together; that's my comfort.

FOIBLE.

Indeed, madam, and so 'tis a comfort if you knew all. He has been even with your ladyship; which I could have 80 told you long enough since, but I love to keep peace and quietness by my good will. I had rather bring friends together than set 'em at distance. But Mrs. Marwood and he are nearer related than ever their parents thought for.

MRS. FAINALL.

Say'st thou so, Foible? Canst thou prove this? 85

FOIBLE.

I can take my oath of it, madam; so can Mrs. Mincing. We have had many a fair word from Madam Marwood, to conceal something that passed in our chamber one evening when you were at Hyde Park and we were thought to have gone a-walking; but we went up unawares, though we were 90 sworn to secrecy too. Madam Marwood took a book and swore us upon it, but it was a book of verses and poems. So as long as it was not a Bible oath, we may break it with a safe conscience.

MRS. FAINALL.

This discovery is the most opportune thing I could wish. 95 Now, Mincing?

---

92. verses and poems] *Q1;* verses   92–93. So as long as] *Q1;* so long
and *omitted in W1.*   as *Q2, W1.*

Enter Mincing.

MINCING.

My lady would speak with Mrs. Foible, mem. Mr. Mirabell
is with her; he has set your spouse at liberty, Mrs. Foible,
and would have you hide yourself in my lady's closet till my
old lady's anger is abated. Oh, my old lady is in a perilous 100
passion at something Mr. Fainall has said; he swears, and
my old lady cries. There's a fearful hurricane, I vow. He
says, mem, how that he'll have my lady's fortune made
over to him, or he'll be divorced.

MRS. FAINALL.

Does your lady or Mirabell know that?   105

MINCING.

Yes, mem; they have sent me to see if Sir Wilfull be sober
and to bring him to them. My lady is resolved to have him,
I think, rather than lose such a vast sum as six thousand
pound. Oh, come, Mrs. Foible, I hear my old lady.

MRS. FAINALL.

Foible, you must tell Mincing that she must prepare to vouch 110
when I call her.

FOIBLE.

Yes, yes, madam.

MINCING.

O yes, mem, I'll vouch anything for your ladyship's service,
be what it will.   *Exeunt* Mincing *and* Foible.

Enter Lady Wishfort *and* Marwood.

LADY WISHFORT.

O my dear friend, how can I enumerate the benefits that 115
I have received from your goodness? To you I owe the
timely discovery of the false vows of Mirabell; to you the
detection of the imposter Sir Rowland. And now you are
become an intercessor with my son-in-law, to save the honor
of my house, and compound for the frailties of my daughter. 120
Well, friend, you are enough to reconcile me to the bad

---

105. or] *W1; and Q1.*   to you I owe the detection *W1.*
117–118. to you the detection] *Q1;*

120. *compound*] make composition.

world, or else I would retire to deserts and solitudes, and
feed harmless sheep by groves and purling streams. Dear
Marwood, let us leave the world, and retire by ourselves and
be shepherdesses. 125

MRS. MARWOOD.

Let us first dispatch the affair in hand, madam. We shall
have leisure to think of retirement afterwards. Here is one
who is concerned in the treaty.

LADY WISHFORT.

O daughter, daughter, is it possible thou shouldst be my
child, bone of my bone, and flesh of my flesh, and, as I may 130
say, another me, and yet transgress the most minute
particle of severe virtue? It is possible you should lean aside
to iniquity, who have been cast in the direct mold of virtue?
I have not only been a mold but a pattern for you, and a
model for you, after you were brought into the world. 135

MRS. FAINALL.

I don't understand your ladyship.

LADY WISHFORT.

Not understand? Why, have you not been naught? Have
you not been sophisticated? Not understand? Here I am
ruined to compound for your caprices and your cuckoldoms.
I must pawn my plate and my jewels, and ruin my niece, and 140
all little enough.

MRS. FAINALL.

I am wronged and abused, and so are you. 'Tis a false
accusation, as false as hell, as false as your friend there, aye,
or your friend's friend, my false husband.

MRS. MARWOOD.

My friend, Mrs. Fainall? Your husband my friend? What 145
do you mean?

MRS. FAINALL.

I know what I mean, madam, and so do you; and so shall
the world at a time convenient.

MRS. MARWOOD.

I am sorry to see you so passionate, madam. More temper

---

137. *naught*] immoral.   138. *sophisticated*] corrupted.
149. *temper*] equanimity, composure.

would look more like innocence. But I have done. I am 150
sorry my zeal to serve your ladyship and family should admit
of misconstruction, or make me liable to affronts. You will
pardon me, madam, if I meddle no more with an affair in
which I am not personally concerned.

LADY WISHFORT.

O dear friend, I am so ashamed that you should meet with 155
such returns! [*To Mrs. Fainall.*] You ought to ask pardon
on your knees, ungrateful creature; she deserves more from
you than all your life can accomplish. [*To Mrs. Marwood.*]
Oh, don't leave me destitute in this perplexity! No, stick to
me, my good genius.   160

MRS. FAINALL.

I tell you, madam, you're abused. Stick to you? Aye, like a
leech, to suck your best blood; she'll drop off when she's
full. Madam, you shan't pawn a bodkin, nor part with a
brass counter, in composition for me. I defy 'em all. Let 'em
prove their aspersions; I know my own innocence, and dare 165
stand by a trial.   *Exit.*

LADY WISHFORT.

Why, if she should be innocent, if she should be wronged
after all, ha? I don't know what to think—and, I promise
you, her education has been unexceptionable. I may say it;
for I chiefly made it my own care to initiate her very infancy 170
in the rudiments of virtue, and to impress upon her tender
years a young odium and aversion to the very sight of
men—aye, friend, she would ha' shrieked if she had but seen
a man, till she was in her teens. As I'm a person, 'tis true.
She was never suffered to play with a male child, though but 175
in coats; nay, her very babies were of the feminine gender.
Oh, she never looked a man in the face but her own father,
or the chaplain, and him we made a shift to put upon her for
a woman, by the help of his long garments and his sleek face,
till she was going in her fifteen.   180

163. shan't] *Q2, W1;* sha'not *Q1.*   166. stand by] *Q1;* stand *W1.*

---

163. *bodkin*] a pin-shaped ornament used by women to fasten up their
hair.

164. *brass counter*] coin of base metal used as a token of payment.

166. *stand by*] undergo.   176. *babies*] dolls.

178. *made a shift*] used a trick.

MRS. MARWOOD.

'Twas much she should be deceived so long.

LADY WISHFORT.

I warrant you, or she would never have borne to have been
catechized by him; and have heard his long lectures against
singing and dancing, and such debaucheries; and going to
filthy plays, and profane music-meetings, where the lewd 185
trebles squeak nothing but bawdy, and the basses roar
blasphemy. Oh, she would have swooned at the sight or
name of an obscene playbook! And can I think, after all
this, that my daughter can be naught? What, a whore?
And thought it excommunication to set her foot within 190
the door of a playhouse! O my dear friend, I can't believe
it, no, no! As she says, let him prove it, let him prove it.

MRS. MARWOOD.

Prove it, madam? What, and have your name prostituted in
a public court! Yours and your daughter's reputation wor-
ried at the bar by a pack of bawling lawyers! To be ushered 195
in with an *Oyez* of scandal, and have your case opened by an
old fumbling lecher in a quoif like a man midwife; to
bring your daughter's infamy to light; to be a theme for
legal punsters and quibblers by the statute, and become
a jest against a rule of court, where there is no precedent 200
for a jest in any record, not even in Doomsday Book; to
discompose the gravity of the bench, and provoke naughty
interrogatories in more naughty law Latin, while the
good judge, tickled with the proceeding, simpers under a
gray beard, and fidges off and on his cushion as if he had 205
swallowed cantharides, or sat upon cow-itch.

191. my dear friend] *Q1;* dear	*W1.*
friend *W1.*	205. fidges] *Q1;* figes *W1.*
196. *Oyez*] *O Yez Q1;* O Yes *Q2,*	206. sat] *Q1;* sate *Q2, W1.*

196. *Oyez*] Hear ye, a cry used by court-criers to gain silence before
making a proclamation.

197. *quoif*] white cap then worn by a serjeant-at-law.

201. *Doomsday Book*] the record of a survey of the lands of England made
in 1085–1086 by order of William the Conqueror.

205. *fidges*] fidgets.

206. *cantharides*] a preparation of dried beetles used for medicinal
purposes.

206. *cow-itch*] cowhage, a tropical vine, the pods of which are covered
with stinging hairs.

LADY WISHFORT.

Oh, 'tis very hard!

MRS. MARWOOD.

And then to have my young revelers of the Temple take
notes, like prentices at a conventicle; and after, talk it all
over again in commons, or before drawers in an eating 210
house.

LADY WISHFORT.

Worse and worse!

MRS. MARWOOD.

Nay, this is nothing; if it would end here, 'twere well. But
it must, after this, be consigned by the shorthand writers
to the public press; and from thence be transferred to the 215
hands, nay into the throats and lungs of hawkers, with
voices more licentious than the loud flounder-man's, or
the woman that cries gray peas. And this you must hear till
you are stunned; nay, you must hear nothing else for some
days.   220

LADY WISHFORT.

Oh, 'tis insupportable! No, no, dear friend; make it up,
make it up; aye, aye, I'll compound. I'll give up all, myself
and my all, my niece and her all, anything, everything for
composition.

MRS. MARWOOD.

Nay, madam, I advise nothing; I only lay before you, as a 225
friend, the inconveniences which perhaps you have overseen. Here comes Mr. Fainall. If he will be satisfied to
huddle up all in silence, I shall be glad. You must think I
would rather congratulate than condole with you.

Enter Fainall.

LADY WISHFORT.

Aye, aye, I do not doubt it, dear Marwood; no, no, I do 230

209–210. all over] *Q1;* over *W1.*

---

208. *revelers of the Temple*] law students of the Inns of Court.

208–209. *take notes, like prentices at a conventicle*] The apprentices of
dissenting tradesmen were required to take notes on sermons for the benefit
of their employers.

217. *the loud flounder-man's*] A certain street vendor for many years
distinguished himself by his forceful manner of crying flounders in the
streets of London.

226–227. *overseen*] overlooked.

not doubt it.

FAINALL.

Well, madam, I have suffered myself to be overcome by the
importunity of this lady your friend, and am content that
you shall enjoy your own proper estate during life, on
condition you oblige yourself never to marry, under such 235
penalty as I think convenient.

LADY WISHFORT.

Never to marry?

FAINALL.

No more Sir Rowlands; the next imposture may not be so
timely detected.

MRS. MARWOOD.

That condition, I dare answer, my lady will consent to, 240
without difficulty; she has already but too much experienced
the perfidiousness of men. Besides, madam, when we retire
to our pastoral solitude, we shall bid adieu to all other
thoughts.

LADY WISHFORT.

Aye, that's true; but in case of necessity, as of health, or 245
some such emergency—

FAINALL.

Oh, if you are prescribed marriage, you shall be considered;
I will only reserve to myself the power to choose for you.
If your physic be wholesome, it matters not who is your
apothecary. Next, my wife shall settle on me the remainder 250
of her fortune, not made over already; and for her maintenance depend entirely on my discretion.

LADY WISHFORT.

This is most inhumanly savage, exceeding the barbarity of
a Muscovite husband.

FAINALL.

I learned it from his Czarish majesty's retinue, in a winter 255
evening's conference over brandy and pepper, amongst other
secrets of matrimony and policy, as they are at present
practiced in the northern hemisphere. But this must be

---

254. *Muscovite*] Russian.
255. *Czarish majesty's retinue*] Peter the Great had visited England in
1698.

agreed unto, and that positively. Lastly, I will be endowed, in right of my wife, with that six thousand pound, 260
which is the moiety of Mrs. Millamant's fortune in your
possession; and which she has forfeited (as will appear by the
last will and testament of your deceased husband, Sir
Jonathan Wishfort) by her disobedience in contracting
herself against your consent or knowledge, and by refusing 265
the offered match with Sir Wilfull Witwoud, which you,
like a careful aunt, had provided for her.

LADY WISHFORT.

My nephew was *non compos*, and could not make his
addresses.

FAINALL.

I come to make demands. I'll hear no objections.   270

LADY WISHFORT.

You will grant me time to consider?

FAINALL.

Yes, while the instrument is drawing, to which you must
set your hand till more sufficient deeds can be perfected;
which I will take care shall be done with all possible speed.
In the meanwhile, I will go for the said instrument, and 275
till my return you may balance this matter in your own
discretion.   *Exit.*

LADY WISHFORT.

This insolence is beyond all precedent, all parallel. Must
I be subject to this merciless villain?

MRS. MARWOOD.

'Tis severe indeed, madam, that you should smart for 280
your daughter's wantonness.

LADY WISHFORT.

'Twas against my consent that she married this barbarian,
but she would have him, though her year was not out.
—Ah! her first husband, my son Languish, would not have
carried it thus. Well, that was my choice, this is hers; she 285
is matched now with a witness. I shall be mad! Dear

---

268. *non compos*] not in his right mind.

272. *while the instrument is drawing*] while the legal document is being
drawn up.

283. *her year was not out*] her first year of widowhood.

286. *with a witness*] the equivalent of *with a vengeance.*

friend, is there no comfort for me? Must I live to be confis-
cated at this rebel rate? —Here come two more of my
Egyptian plagues, too.

Enter Millamant *and* Sir Wilfull Witwoud.

SIR WILFULL.
    Aunt, your servant.   290

LADY WISHFORT.
    Out, caterpillar, call me not aunt! I know thee not!

SIR WILFULL.
    I confess I have been a little in disguise, as they say.
'Sheart! and I'm sorry for't. What would you have? I hope
I committed no offense, aunt, and, if I did, I am willing to
make satisfaction; and what can a man say fairer? If I   295
have broke anything, I'll pay for't, an it cost a pound. And
so let that content for what's past, and make no more
words. For what's to come, to pleasure you I'm willing to
marry my cousin. So pray let's all be friends; she and I are
agreed upon the matter before a witness.   300

LADY WISHFORT.
    How's this, dear niece? Have I any comfort? Can this
be true?

MILLAMANT.
    I am content to be a sacrifice to your repose, madam; and
to convince you that I had no hand in the plot, as you
were misinformed, I have laid my commands on Mirabell 305
to come in person, and be a witness that I give my hand
to this flower of knighthood; and for the contract that
passed between Mirabell and me, I have obliged him to
make a resignation of it in your ladyship's presence. He is
without, and waits your leave for admittance.   310

LADY WISHFORT.
    Well, I'll swear I am something revived at this testimony of
your obedience; but I cannot admit that traitor. I fear I
cannot fortify myself to support his appearance. He is as

---

288. *at this rebel rate*] in this high-handed manner.
289. *Egyptian plagues*] referring to the ten plagues visited upon Pharaoh,
cf. Exodus 7–12.
291. *caterpillar*] i.e., vile fellow.   292. *in disguise*] intoxicated.

terrible to me as a Gorgon; if I see him, I fear I shall turn to
stone, petrify incessantly.   315

MILLAMANT.

If you disoblige him, he may resent your refusal and insist
upon the contract still. Then 'tis the last time he will be
offensive to you.

LADY WISHFORT.

Are you sure it will be the last time? If I were sure of that!
Shall I never see him again?   320

MILLAMANT.

Sir Willfull, you and he are to travel together, are you not?

SIR WILFULL.

'Sheart, the gentleman's a civil gentleman, aunt; let him
come in. Why, we are sworn brothers and fellow travelers.
We are to be Pylades and Orestes, he and I. He is to be my
interpreter in foreign parts. He has been overseas once 325
already; and with proviso that I marry my cousin, will cross
'em once again, only to bear me company. 'Sheart, I'll call
him in. An I set on't once, he shall come in; and see who'll
hinder him.   *Exit.*

MRS. MARWOOD.

This is precious fooling, if it would pass; but I'll know the 330
bottom of it.

LADY WISHFORT.

O dear Marwood, you are not going?

MRS. MARWOOD.

Not far, madam; I'll return immediately.   *Exit.*

Re-enter Sir Wilfull *and* Mirabell.

SIR WILFULL.

Look up, man, I'll stand by you; 'sbud an she do frown,
she can't kill you; besides—harkee, she dare not frown 335
desperately, because her face is none of her own. 'Sheart,
an she should, her forehead would wrinkle like the coat of a

337. an she should] *Q1;* and she
should *Q2, W1.*

314. *Gorgon*] one of the three mythological sisters whose terrible aspect
turned those who beheld them to stone.
324. *Pylades and Orestes*] Pylades was the devoted friend and traveling
companion of Orestes.

cream cheese; but mum for that, fellow traveler.

MIRABELL.

If a deep sense of the many injuries I have offered to so good
a lady, with a sincere remorse and a hearty contrition, can   340
but obtain the least glance of compassion, I am too happy.
Ah, madam, there was a time! But let it be forgotten. I
confess I have deservedly forfeited the high place I once held,
of sighing at your feet. Nay, kill me not, by turning from me
in disdain. I come not to plead for favor; nay, not for   345
pardon. I am a suppliant only for your pity. I am going
where I never shall behold you more.

SIR WILFULL.

How, fellow traveler! You shall go by yourself then.

MIRABELL.

Let me be pitied first, and afterwards forgotten—I ask
no more.   350

SIR WILFULL.

By'r Lady, a very reasonable request, and will cost you
nothing, aunt. Come, come, forgive and forget, aunt; why
you must, an you are a Christian.

MIRABELL.

Consider, madam, in reality you could not receive much
prejudice; it was an innocent device, though I confess it had   355
a face of guiltiness. It was at most an artifice which love
contrived, and errors which love produces have ever been
accounted venial. At least think it is punishment enough
that I have lost what in my heart I hold most dear, that
to your cruel indignation I have offered up this beauty,   360
and with her my peace and quiet; nay, all my hopes of future
comfort.

SIR WILFULL.

An he does not move me, would I might never be o' the
quorum! An it were not as good a deed as to drink, to
give her to him again, I would I might never take shipping!   365

346. your pity] *Q1;* for pity *W1.*   never be *W1.*
363. might never be] *Q1;* may

338. *mum*] silence.
351. *By'r Lady*] By Our Lady.
363–364. *o' the quorum*] one of the justices of the peace constituting a bench.

Aunt, if you don't forgive quickly, I shall melt, I can tell you that. My contract went no farther than a little mouth-glue, and that's hardly dry; one doleful sigh more from my fellow traveler, and 'tis dissolved.

LADY WISHFORT.

Well, nephew, upon your account—ah, he has a false 370 insinuating tongue! Well, sir, I will stifle my just resentment at my nephew's request. I will endeavor what I can to forget, but on proviso that you resign the contract with my niece immediately.

MIRABELL.

It is in writing and with papers of concern; but I have 375 sent my servant for it, and will deliver it to you, with all acknowledgments for your transcendent goodness.

LADY WISHFORT [aside].

Oh, he has witchcraft in his eyes and tongue! When I did not see him, I could have bribed a villain to his assassination; but his appearance rakes the embers which have so long 380 lain smothered in my breast.

Enter Fainall *and* Mrs. Marwood.

FAINALL.

Your date of deliberation, madam, is expired. Here is the instrument; are you prepared to sign?

LADY WISHFORT.

If I were prepared, I am not empowered. My niece exerts a lawful claim, having matched herself by my direction to 385 Sir Wilfull.

FAINALL.

That sham is too gross to pass on me, though 'tis imposed on you, madam.

MILLAMANT.

Sir, I have given my consent.

MIRABELL.

And, sir, I have resigned my pretensions.   390

SIR WILFULL.

And, sir, I assert my right; and will maintain it in defiance of you, sir, and of your instrument. 'Sheart, an you talk of an

---

367. *a little mouth-glue*] an oral promise.

instrument, sir, I have an old fox by my thigh shall hack
your instrument of ram vellum to shreds, sir! It shall not be
sufficient for a mittimus or a tailor's measure. Therefore, 395
withdraw your instrument, sir, or by'r Lady, I shall draw
mine.

LADY WISHFORT.

Hold, nephew, hold!

MILLAMANT.

Good Sir Wilfull, respite your valor.

FAINALL.

Indeed? Are you provided of a guard, with your single 400
beefeater there? But I'm prepared for you, and insist upon
my first proposal. You shall submit your own estate to my
management and absolutely make over my wife's to my sole
use, as pursuant to the purport and tenor of this other
covenant. [*To* Millamant.] I suppose, madam, your con- 405
sent is not requisite in this case; nor, Mr. Mirabell, your
resignation; nor, Sir Wilfull, your right. You may draw your
fox if you please, sir, and make a bear-garden flourish somewhere else; for here it will not avail. This, my Lady Wishfort,
must be subscribed, or your darling daughter's turned 410
adrift, like a leaky hulk, to sink or swim, as she and the
current of this lewd town can agree.

LADY WISHFORT.

Is there no means, no remedy to stop my ruin? Ungrateful
wretch! dost thou not owe thy being, thy subsistence, to
my daughter's fortune?   415

FAINALL.

I'll answer you when I have the rest of it in my possession.

400. a guard] *Q1;* your guard
Q2, W1.

---

393. *fox*] a colloquial term for a sword.
394. *instrument of ram vellum*] legal document, written on parchment
prepared from sheepskin.
395. *mittimus*] warrant of arrest.
395. *tailor's measure*] parchment used by tailors in taking measurements.
399. *respite*] delay.
401. *beefeater*] a yeoman of the royal guard.
408. *bear-garden*] arena for baiting bears.

MIRABELL.

But that you would not accept of a remedy from my hands—
I own I have not deserved you should owe any obligation
to me; or else perhaps I could advise—

LADY WISHFORT.

Oh, what? what? to save me and my child from ruin,   420
from want, I'll forgive all that's past; nay, I'll consent to anything to come, to be delivered from this tyranny.

MIRABELL.

Aye, madam, but that is too late; my reward is inter-
cepted. You have disposed of her who only could have made
me a compensation for all my services. But be it as it may,   425
I am resolved I'll serve you; you shall not be wronged in
this savage manner.

LADY WISHFORT.

How! Dear Mr. Mirabell, can you be so generous at last?
But it is not possible. Harkee, I'll break my nephew's match;
you shall have my niece yet, and all her fortune, if you can   430
but save me from this imminent danger.

MIRABELL.

Will you? I take you at your word. I ask no more. I must
have leave for two criminals to appear.

LADY WISHFORT.

Aye, aye; anybody, anybody!

MIRABELL.

Foible is one, and a penitent.   435

Enter Mrs. Fainall, Foible, *and* Mincing.

MRS. MARWOOD (*to* Fainall).

Oh, my shame! These corrupt things are bought and
brought hither to expose me.

Mirabell *and* Lady Wishfort *go to* Mrs. Fainall *and* Foible.

FAINALL.

If it must all come out, why let 'em know it; 'tis but the
way of the world. That shall not urge me to relinquish or
abate one tittle of my terms; no, I will insist the more.   440

436. bought and] *Q1; omitted in W1.*

FOIBLE.

Yes indeed, madam; I'll take my Bible oath of it.

MINCING.

And so will I, mem.

LADY WISHFORT.

O Marwood, Marwood, art thou false? my friend deceive
me? Hast thou been a wicked accomplice with that pro-
fligate man?   445

MRS. MARWOOD.

Have you so much ingratitude and injustice, to give
credit against your friend to the aspersions of two such
mercenary trulls?

MINCING.

Mercenary, mem? I scorn your words. 'Tis true we found
you and Mr. Fainall in the blue garret; by the same token, 450
you swore us to secrecy upon Messalina's poems. Mercenary?
No, if we would have been mercenary, we should have
held our tongues; you would have bribed us sufficiently.

FAINALL.

Go, you are an insignificant thing! Well, what are you
the better for this? Is this Mr. Mirabell's expedient? I'll be 455
put off no longer. You thing, that was a wife, shall smart
for this! I will not leave thee wherewithal to hide thy
shame; your body shall be as naked as your reputation.

MRS. FAINALL.

I despise you, and defy your malice! You have aspersed
me wrongfully. I have proved your falsehood. Go you and 460
your treacherous—I will not name it, but starve together,
perish!

FAINALL.

Not while you are worth a groat, indeed, my dear. Madam,
I'll be fooled no longer.

LADY WISHFORT.

Ah, Mr. Mirabell, this is small comfort, the detection of this 465
affair.

---

451. *Messalina's poems*] Messalina was the dissolute wife of the Roman
emperor Claudius. Mincing, addicted to malapropisms, may have meant
"miscellaneous."
    463. *groat*] old English coin worth fourpence.

MIRABELL.

Oh, in good time. Your leave for the other offender and penitent to appear, madam.

Enter Waitwell *with a box of writings.*

LADY WISHFORT.

O Sir Rowland! Well, rascal?

WAITWELL.

What your ladyship pleases. I have brought the black 470 box at last, madam.

MIRABELL.

Give it to me. Madam, you remember your promise.

LADY WISHFORT.

Aye, dear sir.

MIRABELL.

Where are the gentlemen?

WAITWELL.

At hand, sir, rubbing their eyes; just risen from sleep.   475

FAINALL.

'Sdeath, what's this to me? I'll not wait your private concerns.

Enter Petulant *and* Witwoud.

PETULANT.

How now? What's the matter? Whose hand's out?

WITWOUD.

Heyday! what, are you all got together, like players at the end of the last act?   480

MIRABELL.

You may remember, gentlemen, I once requested your hands as witnesses to a certain parchment.

WITWOUD.

Aye, I do; my hand I remember. Petulant set his mark.

MIRABELL.

You wrong him; his name is fairly written, as shall appear. You do not remember, gentlemen, anything of what that 485 parchment contained?   *Undoing the box.*

WITWOUD.

No.

---

478. *Whose hand's out?*] Who is making trouble?

PETULANT.

 Not I. I writ. I read nothing.

MIRABELL.

 Very well; now you shall know. Madam, your promise.

LADY WISHFORT.

 Aye, aye, sir, upon my honor.   490

MIRABELL.

 Mr. Fainall, it is now time that you should know that your lady, while she was at her own disposal, and before you had by your insinuations wheedled her out of a pretended settlement of the greatest part of her fortune—

FAINALL.

 Sir! pretended!   495

MIRABELL.

 Yes, sir. I say that this lady, while a widow, having, it seems, received some cautions respecting your inconstancy and tyranny of temper, which from her own partial opinion and fondness of you she could never have suspected—she did, I say, by the wholesome advice of friends and of sages 500 learned in the laws of this land, deliver this same as her act and deed to me in trust, and to the uses within mentioned. You may read if you please (*Holding out the parchment.*)— though perhaps what is inscribed on the back may serve your occasions.   505

FAINALL.

 Very likely, sir. What's here? Damnation! (*Reads.*) "A deed of conveyance of the whole estate real of Arabella Languish, widow, in trust to Edward Mirabell." Confusion!

MIRABELL.

 Even so, sir; 'tis the way of the world, sir, of the widows of 510 the world. I suppose this deed may bear an elder date than what you have obtained from your lady.

FAINALL.

 Perfidious fiend! then thus I'll be revenged.

      Offers to run at Mrs. Fainall.

504. inscribed on] *Q1;* written on *W1.*

SIR WILFULL.

Hold, sir! Now you may make your bear-garden flourish
somewhere else, sir.   515

FAINALL.

Mirabell, you shall hear of this, sir; be sure you shall. Let me
pass, oaf!   *Exit.*

MRS. FAINALL.

Madam, you seem to stifle your resentment; you had better
give it vent.

MRS. MARWOOD.

Yes, it shall have vent, and to your confusion; or I'll perish 520
in the attempt.   *Exit.*

LADY WISHFORT.

O daughter, daughter, 'tis plain thou hast inherited thy
mother's prudence.

MRS. FAINALL.

Thank Mr. Mirabell, a cautious friend, to whose advice all
is owing.   525

LADY WISHFORT.

Well, Mr. Mirabell, you have kept your promise, and I
must perform mine. First, I pardon, for your sake, Sir Rowland there and Foible. The next thing is to break the
matter to my nephew, and how to do that—

MIRABELL.

For that, madam, give yourself no trouble; let me have 530
your consent. Sir Wilfull is my friend; he has had compassion upon lovers, and generously engaged a volunteer
in this action for our service, and now designs to prosecute
his travels.

SIR WILFULL.

'Sheart, aunt, I have no mind to marry. My cousin's a fine 535
lady, and the gentleman loves her, and she loves him, and
they deserve one another; my resolution is to see foreign
parts. I have set on't, and when I'm set on't, I must do't.
And if these two gentlemen would travel too, I think they
may be spared.   540

PETULANT.

For my part, I say little; I think things are best off or on.

---

541. *off or on*] either way.

WITWOUD.

I gad, I understand nothing of the matter; I'm in a maze
yet, like a dog in a dancing school.

LADY WISHFORT.

Well, sir, take her, and with her all the joy I can give you.

MILLAMANT.

Why does not the man take me? Would you have me give 545
myself to you over again?

MIRABELL.

Aye, and over and over again; for I would have you as
often as possibly I can. (*Kisses her hand.*) Well, heaven
grant I love you not too well; that's all my fear.

SIR WILFULL.

'Sheart, you'll have time enough to toy after you're 550
married; or if you will toy now, let us have a dance in the
meantime, that we who are not lovers may have some other
employment besides looking on.

MIRABELL.

With all my heart, dear Sir Wilfull. What shall we do for
music?   555

FOIBLE.

Oh, sir, some that were provided for Sir Rowland's entertainment are yet within call.

A dance.

LADY WISHFORT.

As I am a person, I can hold out no longer. I have wasted
my spirits so today already that I am ready to sink under the
fatigue; and I cannot but have some fears upon me yet that 560
my son Fainall will pursue some desperate course.

MIRABELL.

Madam, disquiet not yourself on that account; to my
knowledge his circumstances are such, he must of force
comply. For my part, I will contribute all that in me lies
to a reunion. In the meantime, madam   (*To* Mrs. Fainall.), 565

---

547. for] *Q1; omitted in Q2, W1.*   you'll have him time enough *Q1.*
550. you'll have time enough] *W1;*

---

542. *I gad*] i.e., by God.
550. *toy*] play.
563. *of force*] necessarily.

let me before these witnesses restore to you this deed of trust;
it may be a means, well-managed, to make you live easily
together.

    From hence let those be warned, who mean to wed,
    Lest mutual falsehood stain the bridal bed;   570
    For each deceiver to his cost may find,
    That marriage frauds too oft are paid in kind.

Exeunt omnes.

EPILOGUE
Spoken by Mrs. Bracegirdle

After our Epilogue this crowd dismisses,
I'm thinking how this play'll be pulled to pieces.
But pray consider, ere you doom its fall,
How hard a thing 'twould be to please you all.
There are some critics so with spleen diseased,   5
They scarcely come inclining to be pleased;
And sure he must have more than mortal skill,
Who pleases any one against his will.
Then, all bad poets we are sure are foes,
And how their number's swelled, the town well knows;   10
In shoals I've marked 'em judging in the pit;
Though they're on no pretense for judgment fit,
But that they have been damned for want of wit.
Since when, they, by their own offenses taught,
Set up for spies on plays, and finding fault.   15
Others there are whose malice we'd prevent;
Such who watch plays with scurrilous intent
To mark out who by characters are meant.
And though no perfect likeness they can trace,
Yet each pretends to know the copied face.   20
These with false glosses feed their own ill nature,
And turn to libel what was meant a satire.
May such malicious fops this fortune find,
To think themselves alone the fools designed;
If any are so arrogantly vain,   25
To think they singly can support a scene,
And furnish fool enough to entertain.
For well the learned and the judicious know
That satire scorns to stoop so meanly low
As any one abstracted fop to show.   30
For, as when painters form a matchless face,
They from each fair one catch some different grace;
And shining features in one portrait blend,

2. I'm *Q2, W1;* In *Q1.*

---

21. *glosses*] notes of explanation.
30. *abstracted*] separated from others.

To which no single beauty must pretend;
So poets oft do in one piece expose   35
Whole *belles assemblées* of coquettes and beaux.

---

36. *belles assemblées*] fashionable gatherings.

Appendix

Chronology

Approximate years are indicated by *.

Political and Literary Events	Life and Major Works of Congreve

1631
John Dryden born.

1633
Samuel Pepys born.

1635
Sir George Etherege born.*

1640
Aphra Behn born.

1641
William Wycherley born.*

1642
First Civil War began (ended 1646).
Theaters closed by Parliament.
Thomas Shadwell born.*

1648
Second Civil War.

1649
Execution of Charles I.

1650
Jeremy Collier born.

1651
Hobbes' *Leviathan* published.

1652
First Dutch War began (ended 1654).
Thomas Otway born.

1653
Nathaniel Lee born.*

1656
D'Avenant's *THE SIEGE OF RHODES* performed at Rutland House.

1657
John Dennis born.

1658
Death of Oliver Cromwell.
D'Avenant's *THE CRUELTY OF THE SPANIARDS IN PERU* performed at the Cockpit.

1660
Restoration of Charles II.
Theatrical patents granted to Thomas Killigrew and Sir William D'Avenant, authorizing them to form, respectively, the King's and the Duke of York's Companies.

1661
Cowley's *THE CUTTER OF COLEMAN STREET*.
D'Avenant's *THE SIEGE OF RHODES* (expanded to two parts).

1662
Charter granted to the Royal Society.

1663
Dryden's *THE WILD GALLANT*.
Tuke's *THE ADVENTURES OF FIVE HOURS*.

1664
Sir John Vanbrugh born.
Dryden's *THE RIVAL LADIES*.
Dryden and Howard's *THE INDIAN QUEEN*.
Etherege's *THE COMICAL REVENGE*.

1665
Second Dutch War began (ended 1667).
Great Plague.

Dryden's *THE INDIAN EM-PEROR.*

Orrery's *MUSTAPHA.*

1666
Fire of London.
Death of James Shirley.

1667
Milton's *Paradise Lost* published.
Sprat's *The History of the Royal Society* published.
Dryden's *SECRET LOVE.*

1668
Death of D'Avenant.
Dryden made Poet Laureate.
Dryden's *An Essay of Dramatic Poesy* published.
Shadwell's *THE SULLEN LOVERS.*

1669
Pepys terminated his diary.
Susannah Centlivre born.

1670
Dryden's *THE CONQUEST OF GRANADA*, Part I.

Born on January 24 at Bardsey, near Leeds, Yorkshire.

1671
Dorset Garden Theatre (Duke's Company) opened.
Colley Cibber born.
Milton's *Paradise Regained* and *Samson Agonistes* published.
Dryden's *THE CONQUEST OF GRANADA*, Part II.
THE REHEARSAL, by the Duke of Buckingham and others.
Wycherley's *LOVE IN A WOOD.*

1672
Third Dutch War began (ended 1674).
Joseph Addison born.
Richard Steele born.
Dryden's *MARRIAGE À LA MODE.*

1674–1681

Lived at Youghal and Carrickfergus in Ireland.

1674
New Drury Lane Theatre (King's Company) opened.
Death of Milton.
Nicholas Rowe born.
Thomas Rymer's *Reflections on Aristotle's Treatise of Poesy* (translation of Rapin) published.
1675
Dryden's *AURENG-ZEBE*.
Wycherley's *THE COUNTRY WIFE*.*
1676
Etherege's *THE MAN OF MODE*.
Otway's *DON CARLOS*.
Shadwell's *THE VIRTUOSO*.
Wycherley's *THE PLAIN DEALER*.
1677
Dryden's *ALL FOR LOVE*.
Lee's *THE RIVAL QUEENS*.
1678
Popish Plot.
George Farquhar born.
Bunyan's *Pilgrim's Progress* (Part I) published.
Rymer's *Tragedies of the Last Age Considered* published.
1679
Exclusion Bill introduced.
Death of Thomas Hobbes.
Death of Roger Boyle, Earl of Orrery.
Charles Johnson born.
1680
Death of Samuel Butler.
Death of John Wilmot, Earl of Rochester.
Dryden's *THE SPANISH FRIAR*.
Lee's *LUCIUS JUNIUS BRUTUS*.
Otway's *THE ORPHAN*.

1681

Charles II dissolved Parliament at Oxford.

Dryden's *Absalom and Achitophel* published.

Tate's adaptation of *KING LEAR*.

1682

The King's and the Duke of York's Companies merged into the United Company.

Dryden's *The Medal, MacFlecknoe,* and *Religio Laici* published.

Otway's *VENICE PRESERVED*.

Entered Kilkenny School, Kilkenny.

1683

Rye House Plot.

Death of Thomas Killigrew.

1685

Death of Charles II; accession of James II.

Revocation of the Edict of Nantes.

The Duke of Monmouth's Rebellion.

Death of Otway.

John Gay born.

Crowne's *SIR COURTLY NICE*.

Dryden's *ALBION AND ALBANIUS*.

1686

On April 5, entered Trinity College, Dublin.

1687

Death of the Duke of Buckingham.

Dryden's *The Hind and the Panther* published.

Newton's *Principia* published.

1688

The Revolution.

Alexander Pope born.

Shadwell's *THE SQUIRE OF ALSATIA*.

Returned to England.

1689

The War of the League of Augsburg began (ended 1697).

Toleration Act.

Death of Aphra Behn.
Shadwell made Poet Laureate.
Dryden's *DON SEBASTIAN*.
Shadwell's *BURY FAIR*.

1690
Battle of the Boyne.
Locke's *Two Treatises of Government* and *An Essay concerning Human Understanding* published.

Visited Ireland.

1691
Death of Etherege.
Langbaine's *An Account of the Dramatic Poets* published.

Enrolled on March 17 as law student in the Middle Temple, London.

1692
Death of Lee.
Death of Shadwell.
Tate made Poet Laureate.

Published a romance, *Incognita*. Contributed poems to Charles Gildon's *Miscellany of Original Poems*. Translated the eleventh satire of Juvenal for Dryden's translation of *The Satires of Juvenal and Persius*.

1693
George Lillo born.
Rymer's *A Short View of Tragedy* published.

THE OLD BACHELOR produced at Drury Lane Theatre in March. *THE DOUBLE DEALER* produced at Drury Lane Theatre in December.

1694
Death of Queen Mary.
Southerne's *THE FATAL MARRIAGE*.

Commemorated the death of Queen Mary in *The Mourning Muse of Alexis*.

1695
Group of actors led by Thomas Betterton leave Drury Lane and establish a new company at Lincoln's Inn Fields.
Southerne's *OROONOKO*.

LOVE FOR LOVE produced at Lincoln's Inn Fields Theatre in April. Appointed Commissioner of Hackney Coaches.
Published essay *Concerning Humour in Comedy*.

1696
Cibber's *LOVE'S LAST SHIFT*.
Vanbrugh's *THE RELAPSE*.

Visited Ireland and received an honorary M.A. degree from Trinity College in February.

1697

Treaty of Ryswick ended the War of the League of Augsburg.
Charles Macklin born.
Vanbrugh's *THE PROVOKED WIFE*.

THE MOURNING BRIDE produced at Lincoln's Inn Fields Theatre in February.

1698

Collier controversy started with the publication of *A Short View of the Immorality and Profaneness of the English Stage*.

Published *Amendments of Mr. Collier's False and Imperfect Citations*.

1699

Farquhar's *THE CONSTANT COUPLE*.

1700

Death of Dryden.
Blackmore's *Satire against Wit* published.

THE WAY OF THE WORLD produced at Lincoln's Inn Fields Theatre in March.
In late summer and autumn, visited Belgium and Holland with Charles Mcin and Jacob Tonson.

1701

Act of Settlement.
War of the Spanish Succession began (ended 1713).
Death of James II.
Rowe's *TAMERLANE*.
Steele's *THE FUNERAL*.

THE JUDGMENT OF PARIS, a masque, performed at Dorset Garden Theatre in March.

1702

Death of William III; accession of Anne.
The Daily Courant began publication.
Cibber's *SHE WOULD AND SHE WOULD NOT*.

1703.

Death of Samuel Pepys.
Rowe's *THE FAIR PENITENT*.

1704

Capture of Gibraltar; Battle of Blenheim.
Defoe's *The Review* began publication (1704–1713).

Collaborated with Vanbrugh and Walsh in *SQUIRE TRELOOBY*, a farce adapted from Molière's *MONSIEUR DE POURCEAUGNAC* and

Swift's *A Tale of a Tub* and *The Battle of the Books* published.
Cibber's *THE CARELESS HUS-BAND.*

1704–1705

1705
Steele's *THE TENDER HUS-BAND.*

1706
Battle of Ramillies.
Farquhar's *THE RECRUITING OFFICER.*

1707
Union of Scotland and England.
Death of Farquhar.
Henry Fielding born.
Farquhar's *THE BEAUX' STRAT-AGEM.*

1708
Downes' *Roscius Anglicanus* published.

1709
Samuel Johnson born.
Rowe's edition of Shakespeare published.
The Tatler began publication (1709–1711).
Centlivre's *THE BUSY BODY.*

1710

1711
Shaftesbury's *Characteristics* published.
The Spectator began publication (1711–1712).
Pope's *An Essay on Criticism* published.

produced at Lincoln's Inn Fields Theatre.

Joint manager with Vanbrugh of the new Haymarket Theatre.

Published *The Tears of Amaryllis.* Appointed Commissioner of Wine Licenses.

Publication of first collected edition of Congreve's works, including *Semele,* an opera.

1713

Treaty of Utrecht ended the War of the Spanish Succession.
Addison's *CATO*.

1714

Death of Anne; accession of George I.

Steele became Governor of Drury Lane.

John Rich assumed management of Lincoln's Inn Fields.

Centlivre's *THE WONDER: A WOMAN KEEPS A SECRET*.

Rowe's *JANE SHORE*.

Appointed an undersearcher of Customs and Secretary to the Island of Jamaica.

1715

Jacobite Rebellion.
Death of Tate.
Rowe made Poet Laureate.
Death of Wycherley.

1716

Addison's *THE DRUMMER*.

1717

David Garrick born.
Cibber's *THE NON-JUROR*.
Gay, Pope, and Arbuthnot's *THREE HOURS AFTER MARRIAGE*.

1718

Death of Rowe.
Centlivre's *A BOLD STROKE FOR A WIFE*.

1719

Death of Addison.
Defoe's *Robinson Crusoe* published.
Young's *BUSIRIS, KING OF EGYPT*.

1720

South Sea Bubble.
Samuel Foote born.
Steele suspended from the Governorship of Drury Lane (restored 1721).
Steele's *The Theatre* (periodical) published.

Pope's translation of Homer's *Iliad* dedicated to Congreve.

Hughes' *THE SIEGE OF DAMAS-CUS*.

1721
Walpole became first Minister.

1722
Steele's *THE CONSCIOUS LOVERS*.

Visited Bath with Henrietta, Duchess of Marlborough, and John Gay.

1723
Death of Susannah Centlivre.
Death of D'Urfey.

Birth on November 23 of Lady Mary Godolphin (afterward Duchess of Leeds), Congreve's daughter by Henrietta, Duchess of Marlborough.

1725
Pope's edition of Shakespeare published.

Made his will on February 26, leaving most of his estate to Henrietta, Duchess of Marlborough.

1726
Death of Jeremy Collier.
Death of Vanbrugh.
Law's *Unlawfulness of Stage Entertainments* published.
Swift's *Gulliver's Travels* published.

Visited by Voltaire.

1727
Death of George I; accession of George II.
Death of Sir Isaac Newton.
Arthur Murphy born.

1728
Pope's *Dunciad* published.
Cibber's *THE PROVOKED HUSBAND* (expansion of Vanbrugh's fragment *A JOURNEY TO LONDON*).
Gay's *THE BEGGAR'S OPERA*.

Wrote *Letter to Viscount Cobham*. In Bath from May through October with Henrietta, Duchess of Marlborough, and Lady Mary Godolphin.

1729
Goodman's Fields Theatre opened.
Death of Steele.
Edmund Burke born.

Died on January 19 in his London lodgings in Surrey Street, off the Strand.
Buried on January 26 in Westminster Abbey.

1730

Cibber made Poet Laureate.

Oliver Goldsmith born.

Thomson's *The Seasons* published.

Fielding's *THE AUTHOR'S FARCE*.

Fielding's *TOM THUMB* (revised as *THE TRAGEDY OF TRAGEDIES*, 1731).

1731

Death of Defoe.

Lillo's *THE LONDON MERCHANT*.

1732

Covent Garden Theatre opened.

Death of Gay.

George Colman the elder born.

Fielding's *THE COVENT-GARDEN TRAGEDY*.

Fielding's *THE MODERN HUSBAND*.

Charles Johnson's *CAELIA*.

1733

Pope's *An Essay on Man* published.

1734

Death of Dennis.

The Prompter began publication (1734–1736).

Theobald's edition of Shakespeare published.

Fielding's *DON QUIXOTE IN ENGLAND*.

1736

Fielding led the "Great Mogul's Company of Comedians" at the Little Theatre in the Haymarket (1736–1737).

Fielding's *PASQUIN*.

Lillo's *THE FATAL CURIOSITY*.

1737

The Stage Licensing Act.

Dodsley's *THE KING AND THE MILLER OF MANSFIELD*.

Fielding's *THE HISTORICAL REGISTER for 1736*.